MATH CHALLENGER

DESIGN, SOLVE AND BUILD WITH MATH!

HILARY KOLL AND **STEVE MILLS**

ILLUSTRATED BY
VLADIMIR ALEKSIC

QEB

CONTENTS

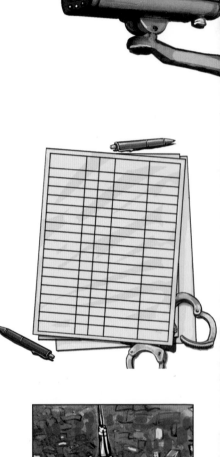

LAUNCH A ROCKET INTO SPACE

FLY A JET FIGHTER

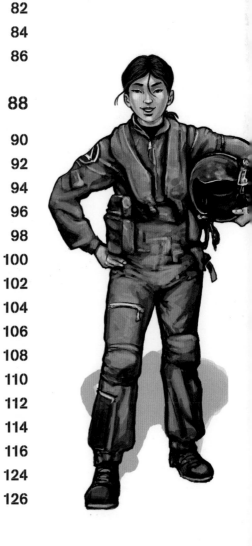

TYPES OF CRIME

You have been chosen to lead a team of detectives who are investigating a burglary at an apartment building.

Crimes are known as criminal offences and there are many different kinds. Two main types are "offences against people" and "offences against property."

Offences against people include assault and robbery. Offences against property include crimes such as arson and burglary.

You are studying a newspaper article showing crime figures from the past 30 years.

Monday May 4, 2015

Falling crime!

It is estimated that there were eight million incidents of crime in the 12 months to the end of September, with violent offences dropping by 13 percent and overall household crime, including burglary, falling by one tenth. Crimes against people were down nine percent. Vehicle theft was down by a quarter. Murders and killings have almost halved in the last decade.

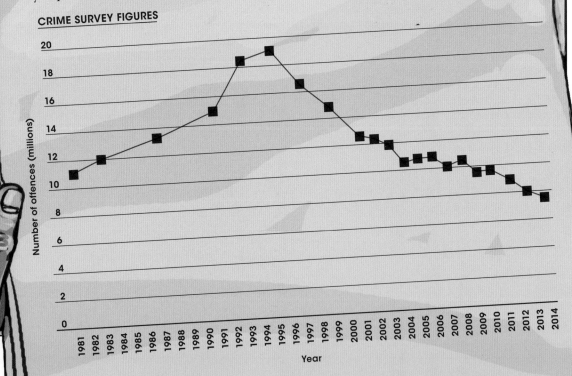

CRIME SURVEY FIGURES

Number of offences (millions) vs Year

1. a) The crime report says that there were eight million incidents of crime. Write eight million in figures.

b) Murders and killings have almost halved. Write one half as a **fraction**, as a **decimal**, and as a **percentage**.

CRIME FALL	FRACTION	DECIMAL	PERCENTAGES
Violent offences	$^{13}/_{100}$	0.13	13%
Murders and killings	$^{1}/_{2}$		
Household crime	$^{1}/_{10}$		
Vehicle theft	$^{1}/_{4}$		
Crimes against people			9%

2. Copy this table and add in the missing fractions, decimals, and percentages.

3. If there were 96,000 vehicle thefts last year and this has gone down by one quarter, how many were there this year?

4. If there were 5,400,000 household crimes last year and this has gone down by 10 percent, how many were there this year?

WHAT ABOUT THIS?
If 20 percent of the eight million incidents were offences against people, and 80 percent of the eight million incidents were offences against property, how many of each type were there?

POLICE DETECTIVES

Your first role is to pick your team of investigators—they'll need to do a number of different jobs from senior officers to regular policemen and women, as well as specialist roles, such as forensic experts.

Those applying to join your team must be in good health and be physically fit.

They should also have a Body Mass Index (BMI) between 18 and 30.

This table shows five people who would like to join your team.

NAME	M/F	WEIGHT	HEIGHT
Dan Archer	Male	160 lb	80 in
Iain Jones	Male	320 lb	80 in
Alice Raven	Female	120 lb	60 in
David Singh	Male	240 lb	80 in
Paula Lee	Female	195 lb	65 in

SCENE OF THE CRIME

After arriving at the apartment, your first job is to cordon off the area so that no one can disturb any evidence.

It's then time to start collecting evidence, taking photographs, and recording statements from anyone who witnessed the crime.

This plan shows the crime scene. A safe located in the victim's living room was broken into.

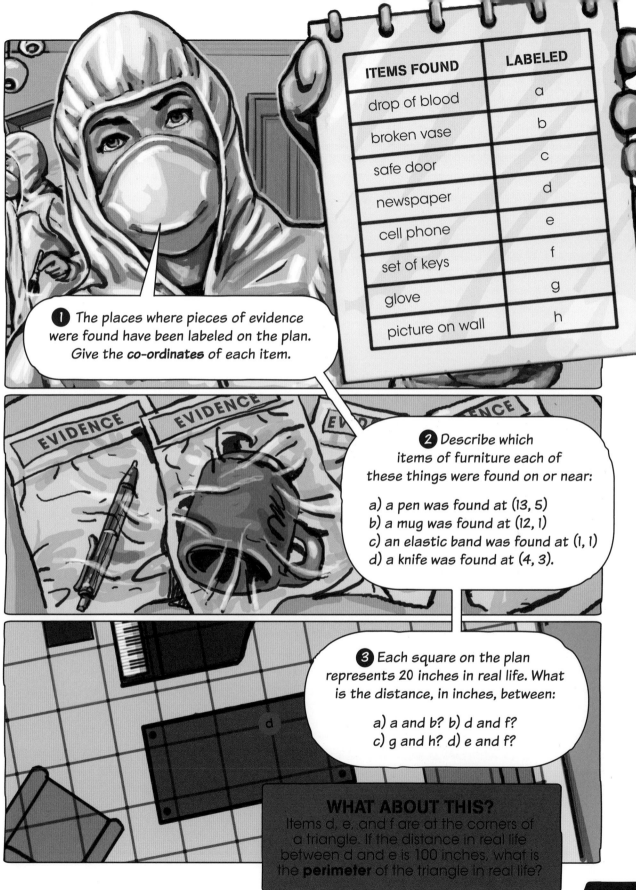

ITEMS FOUND	LABELED
drop of blood	a
broken vase	b
safe door	c
newspaper	d
cell phone	e
set of keys	f
glove	g
picture on wall	h

❶ The places where pieces of evidence were found have been labeled on the plan. Give the **co-ordinates** of each item.

❷ Describe which items of furniture each of these things were found on or near:

a) a pen was found at (13, 5)
b) a mug was found at (12, 1)
c) an elastic band was found at (1, 1)
d) a knife was found at (4, 3).

❸ Each square on the plan represents 20 inches in real life. What is the distance, in inches, between:

a) a and b? b) d and f?
c) g and h? d) e and f?

WHAT ABOUT THIS?
Items d, e, and f are at the corners of a triangle. If the distance in real life between d and e is 100 inches, what is the **perimeter** of the triangle in real life?

FORENSICS AND FINGERPRINTING

Your forensics team arrives at the crime scene to collect detailed evidence. Forensic experts check the scene of the crime to look for fingerprints and other tiny bits of evidence to help identify the criminal.

Fingerprints come in several different types, although no two people have exactly the same prints. Forensic experts brush a light powder over prints to make them visible.

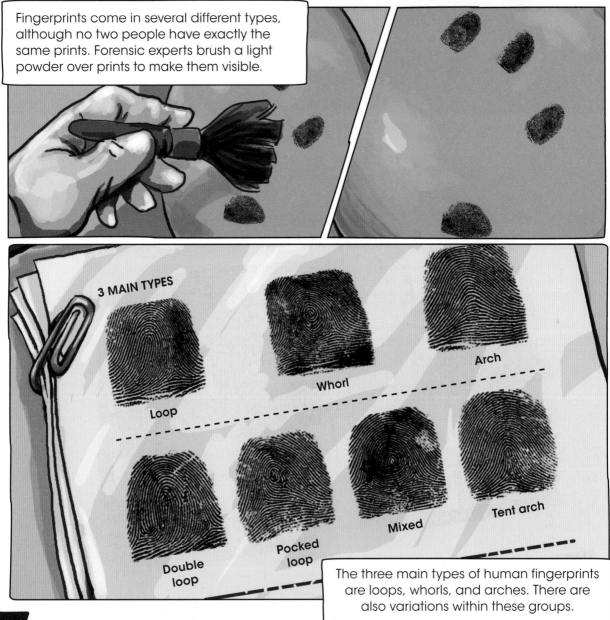

3 MAIN TYPES

Loop

Whorl

Arch

Double loop

Pocked loop

Mixed

Tent arch

The three main types of human fingerprints are loops, whorls, and arches. There are also variations within these groups.

DNA

Your forensic team collects DNA samples from the crime scene. DNA is a spiral-shaped chemical that is found in every cell of the body.

DNA determines how each cell develops. Only a very small number of people have the same DNA, such as identical twins, so it can be very helpful in identifying criminals.

DNA strand

Magnified x 10,000,000

Your forensic experts found a drop of blood at the scene and collected a DNA sample from it. DNA samples can also be collected from hairs or skin cells.

The sample is taken back to a laboratory where the forensic experts can match it against DNA from suspects (people you think committed a crime).

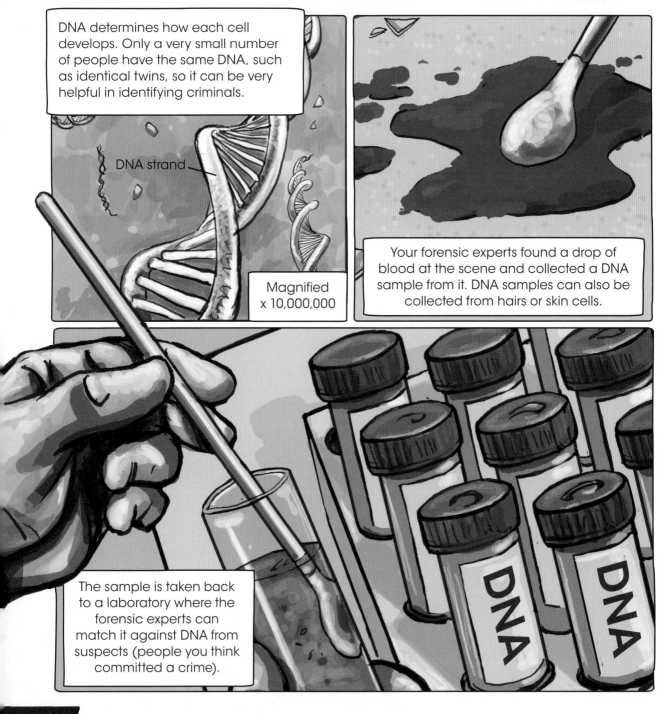

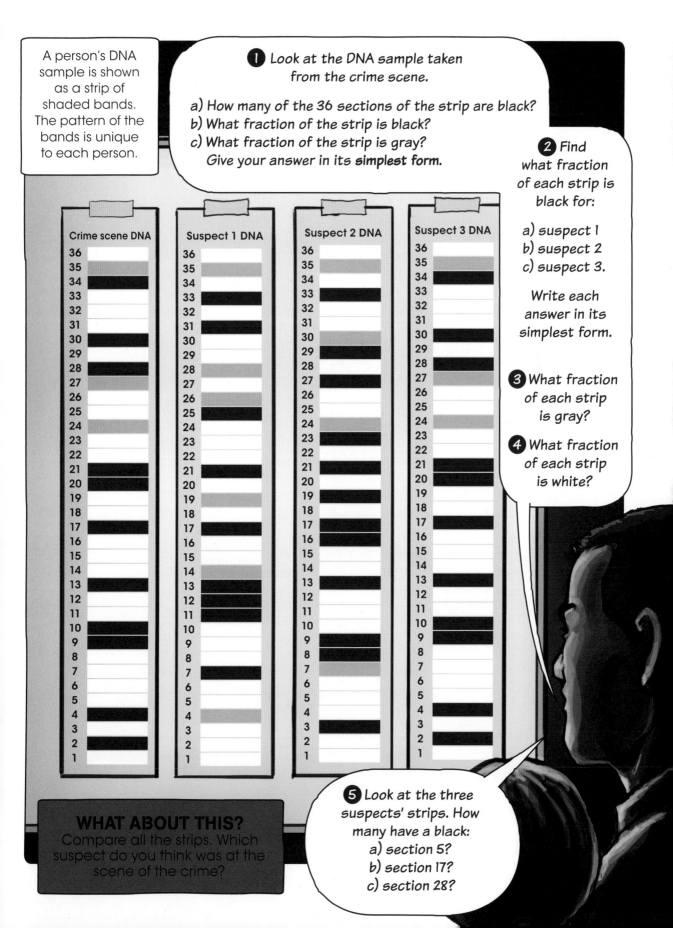

TIMELINES AND ALIBIS

Collecting evidence and taking statements from witnesses allows you to put together a **timeline** of events showing when things happened.

Timelines can help to rule out suspects who have alibis for particular times. An alibi is proof that a person was not at the scene when the crime was committed.

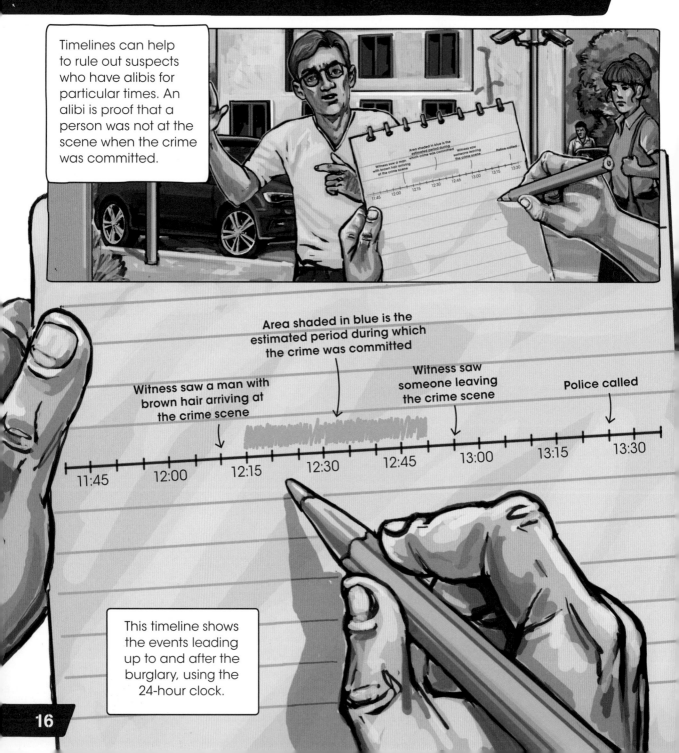

Area shaded in blue is the estimated period during which the crime was committed

Witness saw a man with brown hair arriving at the crime scene

Witness saw someone leaving the crime scene

Police called

11:45　12:00　12:15　12:30　12:45　13:00　13:15　13:30

This timeline shows the events leading up to and after the burglary, using the 24-hour clock.

1 Give your answers using the words "past" or "to." At what time:

a) did the witness see a person arriving at the crime scene?
b) did the witness see a person leaving the crime scene?
c) were the police called?

2 Using the period shown on the timeline, could the crime have been committed at:

a) noon?
b) half past twelve?
c) five minutes past twelve?
d) ten minutes past twelve?
e) twenty minutes to one?
f) five to one?
g) one o'clock?
h) twenty-five past twelve?

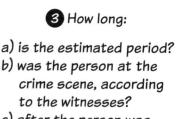

3 How long:

a) is the estimated period?
b) was the person at the crime scene, according to the witnesses?
c) after the person was seen leaving were the police called?

Estimated period during which crime was committed

:15   12:30   12:45

WHAT ABOUT THIS?

Three suspects have alibis that confirm their whereabouts at the following times:

Suspect 1: from eleven-thirty until five to one
Suspect 2: from midday until quarter past one
Suspect 3: from one o'clock until half past two.

Write whether each suspect could have committed the crime based on their alibis.

CAMERA FOOTAGE

One other thing your team must check is the footage from security cameras near the crime scene.

Camera footage is often useful in providing evidence that a person was at or near a crime scene. Detectives will look at video footage from any cameras near the scene.

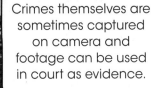

Crimes themselves are sometimes captured on camera and footage can be used in court as evidence.

This plan shows the parking lot outside the apartment building where the burglary took place. The blue shaded sections are the areas covered by the cameras located at 1, 2, 3, 4, and 5.

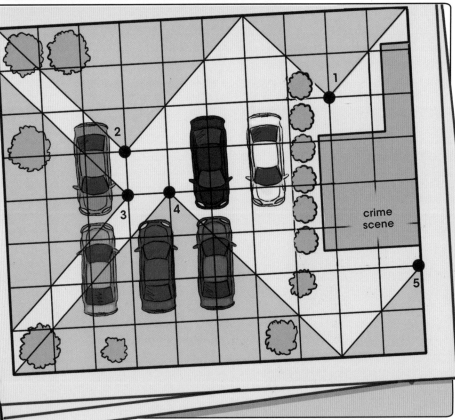

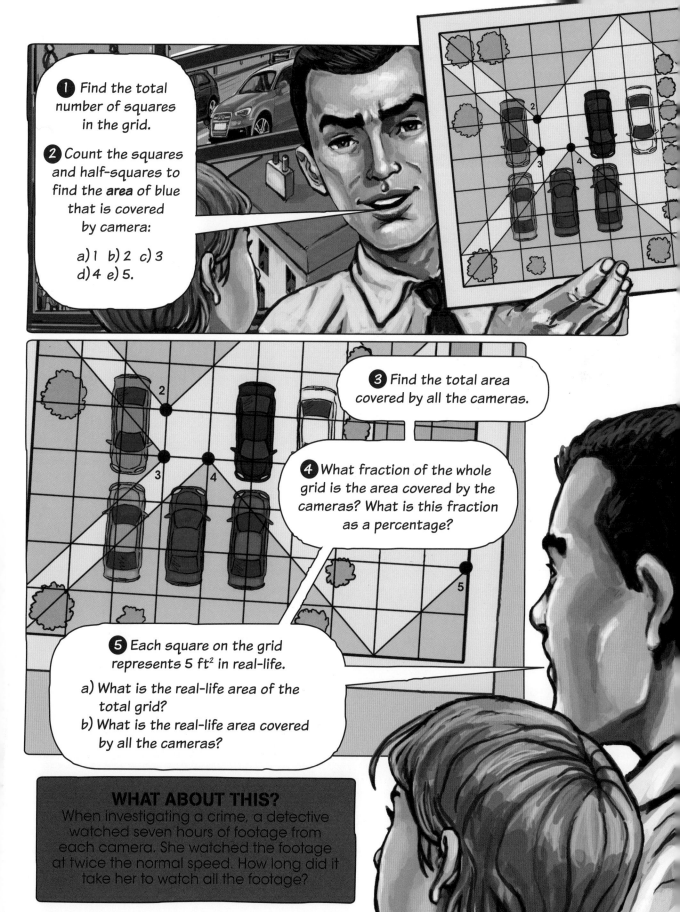

VITAL EVIDENCE

One of your detectives is keeping a record of what has happened and when during the investigation.

This record will help you to keep track of when and where any evidence is found and recorded.

2.00 pm

2.30 pm

4.45 pm

TIME	ACTIVITY
2:00 pm	Arrive at the scene of the burglary
2:15 pm	Secure the perimeter
2:30 pm	Talk to the victims
3:40 pm	Talk to witnesses
4:15 pm	Process scene, including videoing & photographing
4:45 pm	Collect evidence
6:00 pm	Transport evidence for analysis
6:35 pm	Return to police station

This table shows what the detective did during his initial investigation.

TIME	A...
2:00 pm	Arrive at the scene o...
2:15 pm	Secure the perimete...
2:30 pm	Talk to the victims
3:40 pm	Talk to witnesses
4:15 pm	Process scene, incl...
4:45 pm	Collect evidence
6:00 pm	Transport evidenc...
...m	Return to police...

2 Write how many minutes the detective spent from the start of each activity below, to the start of the next activity:

a) securing the perimeter
b) talking to the victims
c) talking to witnesses
d) collecting evidence.

1 Write in words the time (using the words "o"clock," "past," or "to") that the detective:

a) arrived at the scene of the burglary
b) began to talk to witnesses
c) began to collect evidence
d) returned to the police station.

3 What was the detective doing at:

a)

b)

c) 16:05

d) 17:37

WHAT ABOUT THIS?
If the detective began work at 9:00 am and, on returning to the police station after being at the crime scene, he stayed another 25 minutes before finishing work, how many hours did he work in total?

SURVEILLANCE

Surveillance officers watch people or places to gather information to help solve crimes or to get enough evidence for a court case.

You have received a tip-off that the suspect is going to be in a café nearby.

You send an undercover surveillance officer to sit outside the café and record the number of people entering. She estimates the age of each person and makes a note of their hair color.

This is her recording sheet.

GENDER	M	F	F	M	F	F	M	M	M	F	M	F	M	M
AGE	20s	50s	20s	30s	60s	70s	30s	30s	40s	40s	50s	20s	20s	40s
HAIR COLOR	Bl	Br	Blo	Bl	Br	Br	Blo	Rd	Bl	Br	Bl	Bl	Bl	Rd
GENDER	M	M	F	F	F	F	M	M	M	M	F	F	M	F
AGE	80s	40s	60s	20s	50s	70s	30s	40s	50s	30s	40s	20s	30s	60s
HAIR COLOR	Bl	Rd	Br	Rd	Blo	Br	Bl	Br	Br	Br	Bl	Blo	Rd	Br

Key for hair color   Blo = Blonde   Bl = Black   Br = Brown   Rd = Red

MALES		
ESTIMATED AGE	TALLIES	FREQUENCY
20s		
30s		
40s		
50s		
60s		
70s		
80s		

1 The data is reorganized into two frequency tables (one for males and one for females). Copy the table then complete the tallies to find the frequencies.

2 How many males appeared to be:
a) in their 20s? b) in their 70s?
c) in their 50s? d) in their 30s?

FEMALES		
ESTIMATED AGE	TALLIES	FREQUENCY
20s		
30s		
40s		
50s		
60s		
70s		
80s		

3 How many females appeared to be:

a) in their 40s? b) in their 80s?
c) in their 60s? d) in their 20s?

4 How many more males were there than females in total?

WHAT ABOUT THIS?
The tip-off said the suspect was going to the café with a man in his 50s who has brown hair. Describe two possible suspects using the data from the recording sheets.

PROFILING

To help solve your investigation, you turn to the help of a criminal profiler. Trained in human behavior, profilers analyze the evidence from the crime, and make predictions about the characteristics of the unknown criminal.

Profilers look for motives—reasons why someone might commit a crime.

A criminal profiler has said that the suspect is likely to be a man in his 30s, with no educational qualifications, who probably has his own vehicle. You have put together this list of possible suspects.

NAME	SEX	AGE	LEVEL OF EDUCATION	OWNS OWN VEHICLE?
Simon Stone	M	37	None	Y
John Cox	M	34	High School	N
Sam Evans	M	51	Master's	N
Urvi Chandi	M	42	None	Y
James Jones	M	36	None	Y
Mel Mason	M	47	College	Y
Chris Carter	M	37	None	Y
Joe West	M	44	High School	N
Richard Reed	M	48	College	N
Tom Collins	M	39	Master's	Y
Toby Franks	M	50	Master's	N
Ed Lodge	M	42	None	Y
Arthur Holt	M	41	High School	N
Hugh Na	M	63	Master's	Y
Richard Fox	M	53	High School	Y
Paul Raven	M	42	None	N
Larry Jones	M	39	College	Y
Simon Dupa	M	49	High School	Y

E-FITS

With the help of witness statements, your next task is to put together an E-fit, or a picture of the suspect's face, based on the witnesses' recollections.

An E-fit is constructed using computer software to build up different parts of a person's face.

Two witnesses have given you slightly different descriptions of what the suspect may have looked like. You have put together these two E-fits using different eyes, noses, and mouths.

Suspect A

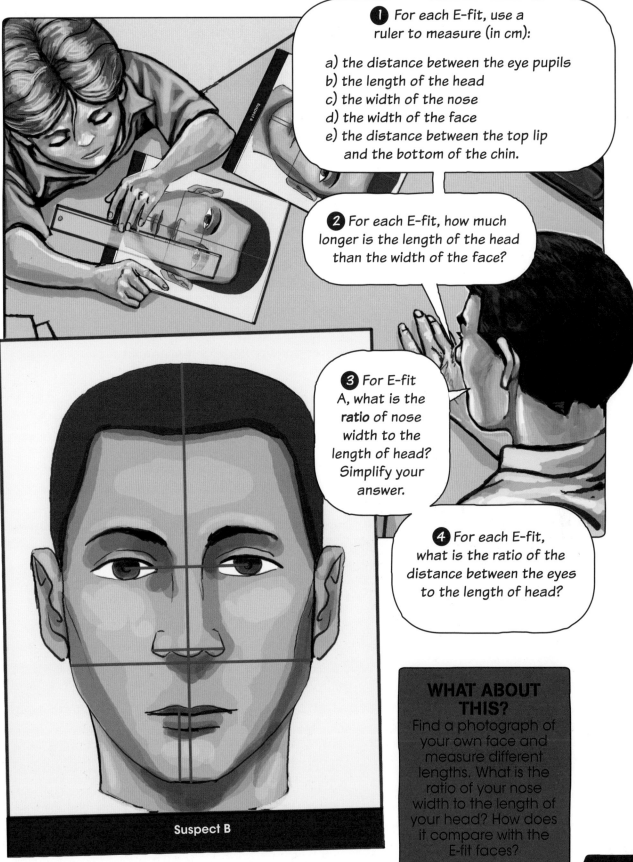

1 For each E-fit, use a ruler to measure (in cm):

a) the distance between the eye pupils
b) the length of the head
c) the width of the nose
d) the width of the face
e) the distance between the top lip and the bottom of the chin.

2 For each E-fit, how much longer is the length of the head than the width of the face?

3 For E-fit A, what is the **ratio** of nose width to the length of head? Simplify your answer.

4 For each E-fit, what is the ratio of the distance between the eyes to the length of head?

Suspect B

WHAT ABOUT THIS?
Find a photograph of your own face and measure different lengths. What is the ratio of your nose width to the length of your head? How does it compare with the E-fit faces?

SOLVING THE CRIME

The victims of the burglary tell the detectives that $1,600 in cash was stolen from the safe.

The detectives decide to check the suspects' bank accounts to see if any large amounts of money have been added.

Sometimes, criminals deposit money in small amounts over several months to avoid suspicion.

1 How much would a suspect deposit altogether if he paid:

a) $300 per month for 3 months?
b) $900 per month for 7 months?
c) $110 per month for a year?
d) $70 per month for 11 months?
e) $80 per month for 18 months?
f) $70 per month for 2 years?

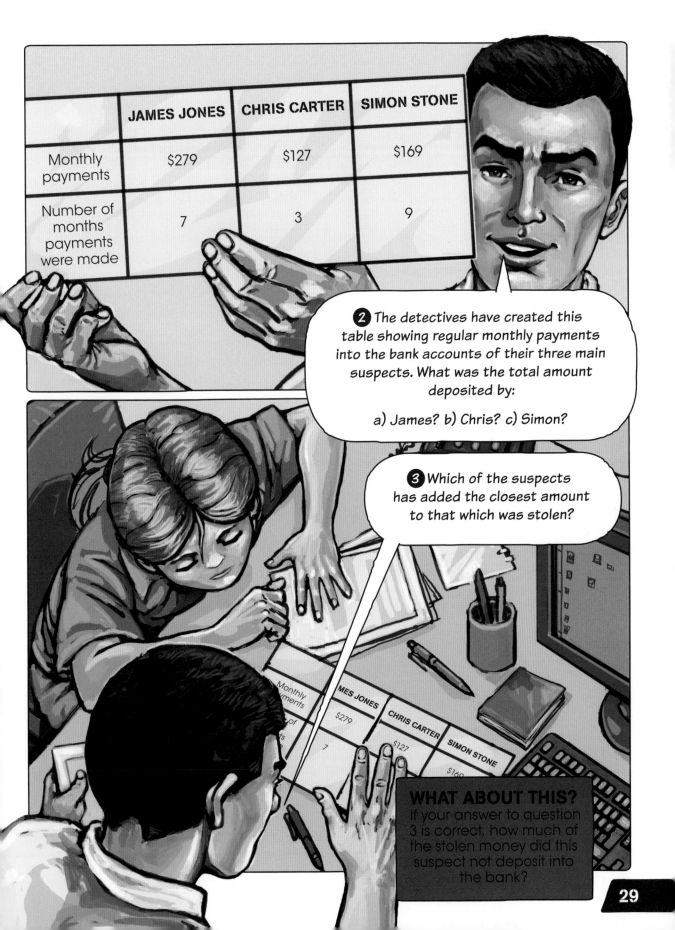

THE ARREST

Your investigation is reaching its climax! DNA tests from the crime scene and other evidence have confirmed the identity of the criminal.

Now that you've solved the crime, it's time to go and arrest him. He has been reported as being in a blue car traveling east along Green Lane (marked with a blue circle below).

Green Lane

C81 M35

ROAD CLOSED   DETOUR

The eastern end of Green Lane is closed due to construction so he's in a traffic jam.

1 You leave the police station parking lot (marked with a P). Describe two different routes to reach the suspect's car (blue circle). Use compass directions in your descriptions.

POLICE

VROOM

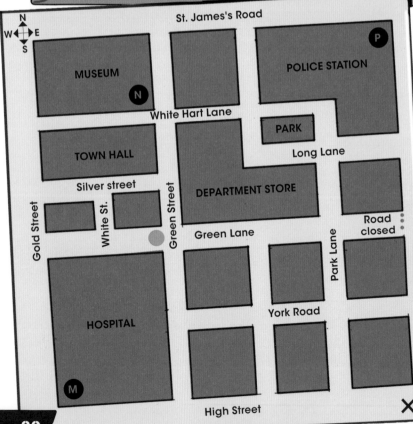

N
W ◄►E
S

St. James's Road

MUSEUM

N

POLICE STATION

P

White Hart Lane

PARK

TOWN HALL

Long Lane

Silver street

White St.

Green Street

DEPARTMENT STORE

Gold Street

Green Lane

Park Lane

Road closed

York Road

HOSPITAL

M

High Street

✕

2 You reach the suspect's car, but it's parked and he's escaped on foot! You know that the suspect owns a storeroom (marked N) near the Museum. How many different routes are there to get from the blue circle to N using only streets with a color in their name.

3 You receive a tip-off that the suspect ran north along Green Street and then east along White Hart Lane. Where could he be hiding?

You're still inspecting the car but you're told that the suspect's moved again and he's now running along the eastern end of High Street. You rush to make the arrest (at the black cross).

4 How many different routes are there from the blue circle to the black cross, avoiding the closed road?

Arriving at the end of High Street, you spot the criminal and make the arrest!

WHAT ABOUT THIS?
The suspect is first taken to the hospital for treatment to a cut and is then taken to the police station to be charged. Are there more or fewer than 20 possible routes from M to P on the map?

>YOU+DO-THE÷MATH

DESIGN A SKYSCRAPER

SHAPES OF SKYSCRAPERS

You have been asked to design a towering skyscraper using the latest designs and cutting-edge technology and materials.

Skyscrapers come in lots of different shapes and sizes.

These shapes include cylinders, cuboids, **prisms**, **pyramids**, and cones, or a combination of these.

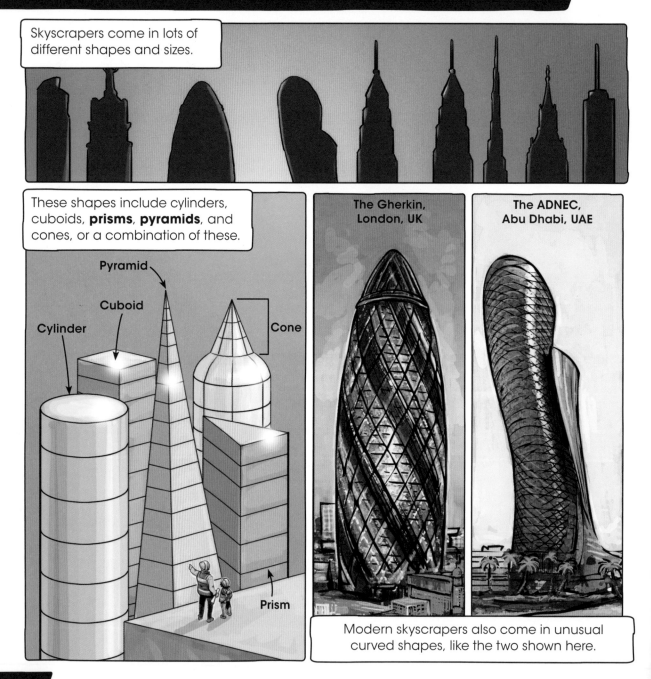

Pyramid

Cuboid

Cylinder

Cone

Prism

The Gherkin, London, UK

The ADNEC, Abu Dhabi, UAE

Modern skyscrapers also come in unusual curved shapes, like the two shown here.

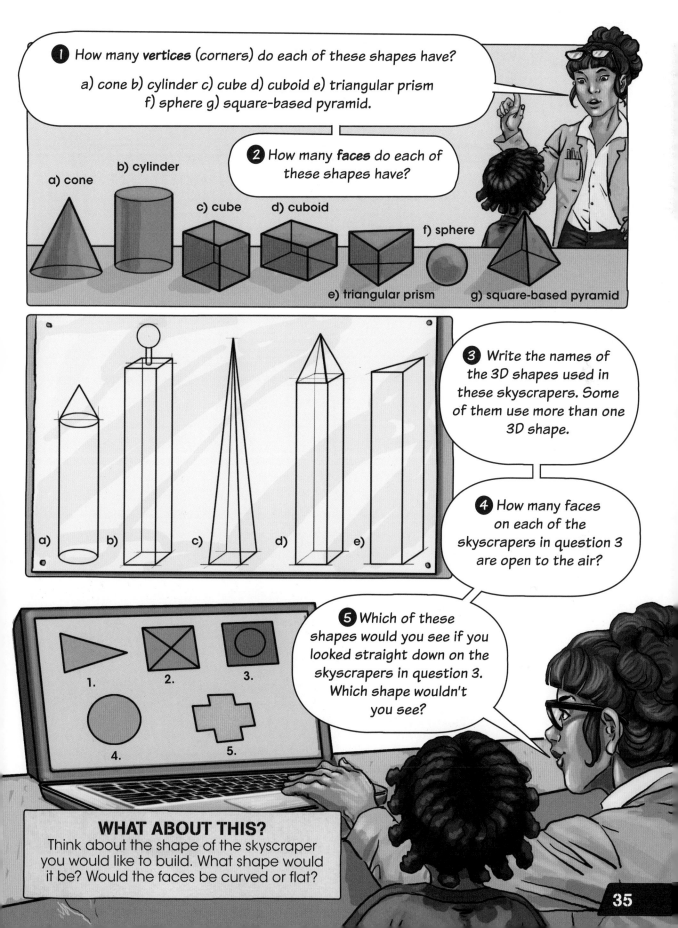

1. How many **vertices** (corners) do each of these shapes have?

a) cone b) cylinder c) cube d) cuboid e) triangular prism f) sphere g) square-based pyramid.

2. How many **faces** do each of these shapes have?

a) cone
b) cylinder
c) cube
d) cuboid
e) triangular prism
f) sphere
g) square-based pyramid

3. Write the names of the 3D shapes used in these skyscrapers. Some of them use more than one 3D shape.

a) b) c) d) e)

4. How many faces on each of the skyscrapers in question 3 are open to the air?

5. Which of these shapes would you see if you looked straight down on the skyscrapers in question 3. Which shape wouldn't you see?

1. 2. 3. 4. 5.

WHAT ABOUT THIS?
Think about the shape of the skyscraper you would like to build. What shape would it be? Would the faces be curved or flat?

35

THE SIZE OF SKYSCRAPERS

New skyscrapers are being built all the time with the aim of being the tallest in the world. When one becomes the tallest, an even taller one is planned!

You have been asked to make your skyscraper one of the tallest in the world. You are looking at other tall buildings around the globe to see how yours will compare.

Makkah Royal Clock Tower, Saudi Arabia: 1,972 ft

One World Trade Center, USA: 1,776 ft

Big Ben, UK: 315 ft

Empire State Building, USA: 1,250 ft

Shanghai Tower, China: 2,073 ft

Petronas Twin Towers, Malaysia: 1,482 ft

Burj Khalifa, UAE: 2,722 ft

This table shows the heights of some famous buildings, including some of the tallest towers on the planet.

NAME	COUNTRY	HEIGHT
Big Ben	UK	315 ft
The Shard	UK	1,017 ft
The Gherkin	UK	591 ft
Empire State Building	USA	1,250 ft
One World Trade Center	USA	1,776 ft
Petronas Twin Towers	Malaysia	1,482 ft
Taipei 101 Tower	Taiwan	1,670 ft
Jin Mao Building	China	1,381 ft
Burj Khalifa	UAE	2,722 ft
Shanghai Tower	China	2,073 ft
Makkah Royal Clock Tower	Saudi Arabia	1,972 ft

1 How much taller is:

a) the Shard than the Gherkin?
b) the Jin Mao Building than the Empire State Building?
c) Burj Khalifa than Big Ben?

2 List the buildings in order of height from shortest to tallest.

Empire State Building, USA: 1,250 ft

3 Which building is:

a) 101 feet taller than the Makkah Royal Clock Tower?
b) 395 feet taller than the Jin Mao Building?
c) 653 feet shorter than the Taipei 101 Tower?

4 Round the height of each building to the nearest 100 feet.

WHAT ABOUT THIS?
Find out the heights of the tallest buildings in the world before 1880 and create a table listing them in height order.

RECORD-BREAKING SKYSCRAPERS

As part of your research into other tall buildings, you have been looking into the history of skyscrapers.

The term "skyscraper" was first used for a tall building in the 1880s.

This graph shows the heights of the tallest skyscrapers for the first year of each decade since the 1880s.

The Home Insurance Building in Chicago, USA, was built in 1884 and is considered the world's first skyscraper.

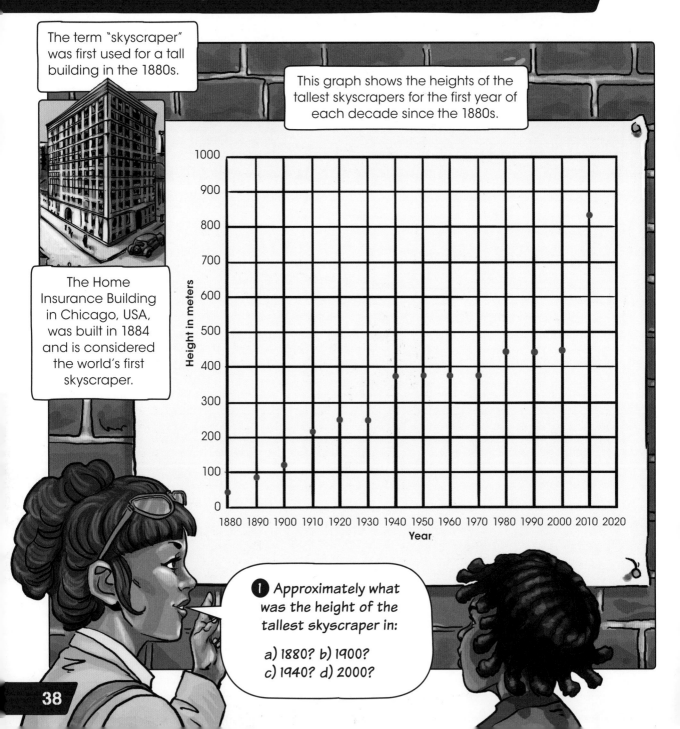

1 Approximately what was the height of the tallest skyscraper in:

a) 1880? b) 1900?
c) 1940? d) 2000?

2 The Empire State Building was the tallest building in the world for about 40 years. Use the graph to work out the answers to these questions:

a) In which decade was it built?
b) About how tall is it?
c) Approximately how much taller was the Empire State Building than the tallest skyscraper in 1930?
d) Approximately how much smaller is the Empire State Building than the tallest skyscraper was in 2000?

3 The Petronas Twin Towers in Kuala Lumpur were the first buildings taller than 450 meters. They were the tallest buildings in the world for six years. In which period on the graph were they the tallest?

4 During which decade was there the largest increase in the height of the tallest skyscraper?

WHAT ABOUT THIS?
The Taipei 101 Tower was the tallest skyscraper for six years, measuring 509 meters. Look at the graph. In which decade was it the tallest? Explain why there is not a mark showing its height.

CHOOSING THE SITE

It is important that you choose a good piece of land or site to build your skyscraper on.

You have four sites to choose from and you need to make sure that the one you choose is suitable to build on. Building close to water can mean the foundations have to go deeper, which could be more expensive. Flattening any hills or removing trees may also add problems.

You should also think about the shape of your skyscraper and whether it will fit.

Key

Building outline | Tree | Hill | River | Lake

SECURING THE SITE

Once the site has been cleared, you'll need to fence it off for security and safety reasons before building work can begin.

The fence around the edge of the site is known as the perimeter fence.

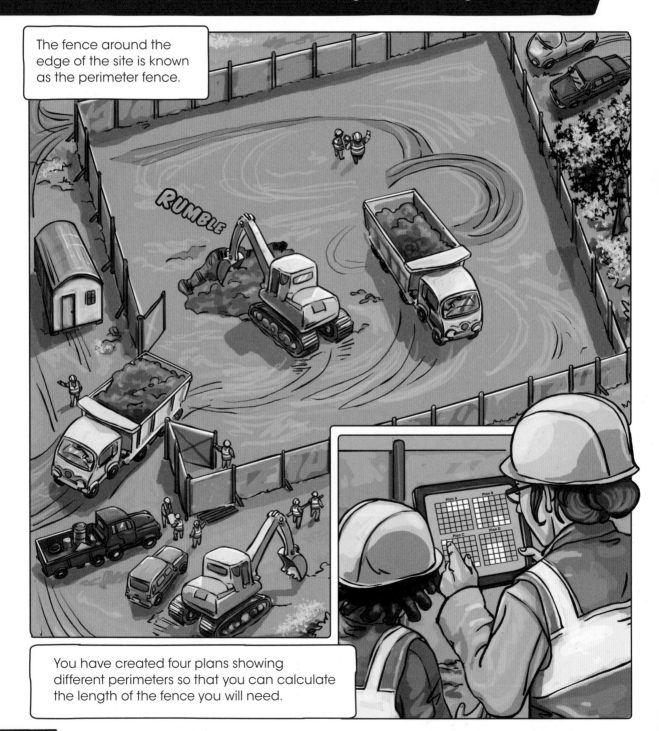

You have created four plans showing different perimeters so that you can calculate the length of the fence you will need.

In these plans, the length of one side of each square represents 10 feet.

Plan A

Plan B

↕ 10 ft

Plan C

Plan D

1 Work out the length of the perimeter fence of each plan.

2 Count the squares of each plan.

3 Does the plan with the longest perimeter have the largest area?

4 Each square represents an area of 100 ft². Multiply the number of squares in each plan by 100 to find its area.

5 Is it possible to have two or more plans with the same length perimeter fence but of different areas? Give examples.

WHAT ABOUT THIS?
If the area of the skyscraper you want to build on the site is 25,000 m² and it will have a height of 500 meters, what will be the **volume** of the skyscraper?

DIGGING FOUNDATIONS

Solid foundations are vital if your skyscraper is going to stay up. It is important to dig down until solid ground is reached and put in foundations to support the structure of your building.

Having dug a large hole in the ground, lots of steel bars and concrete are used to spread the weight of the building evenly.

You can use **negative numbers** (numbers below zero) to show how far below ground your foundations will go.

THUNK

❶ A machine digs down through the soil. If it has dug down 2 feet below ground level (–2 feet) and then digs a further 6 feet down, how far below ground level has it dug?

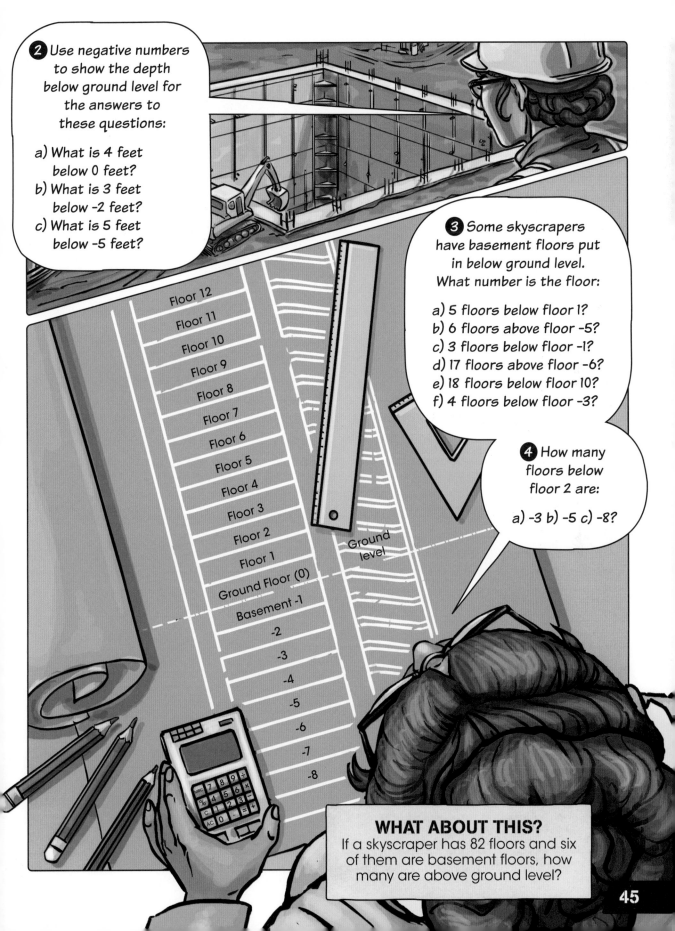

2 Use negative numbers to show the depth below ground level for the answers to these questions:

a) What is 4 feet below 0 feet?
b) What is 3 feet below –2 feet?
c) What is 5 feet below –5 feet?

3 Some skyscrapers have basement floors put in below ground level. What number is the floor:

a) 5 floors below floor 1?
b) 6 floors above floor –5?
c) 3 floors below floor –1?
d) 17 floors above floor –6?
e) 18 floors below floor 10?
f) 4 floors below floor –3?

4 How many floors below floor 2 are:

a) –3 b) –5 c) –8?

Floor 12
Floor 11
Floor 10
Floor 9
Floor 8
Floor 7
Floor 6
Floor 5
Floor 4
Floor 3
Floor 2
Floor 1
Ground Floor (0)
Basement -1
-2
-3
-4
-5
-6
-7
-8

Ground level

WHAT ABOUT THIS?
If a skyscraper has 82 floors and six of them are basement floors, how many are above ground level?

STRONG MATERIALS

With strong foundations in place, the main building work on your skyscraper can begin.

Steel girders are needed to make sure the frame of your skyscraper is strong.

Girders are long prisms and usually have a cross-section that looks like the letters I, H, or T. These shapes are less likely to bend.

❶ The letters I, H, and T are all symmetrical, because they have at least one line of **reflective symmetry**. Which of the other capital letters in our alphabet are symmetrical?

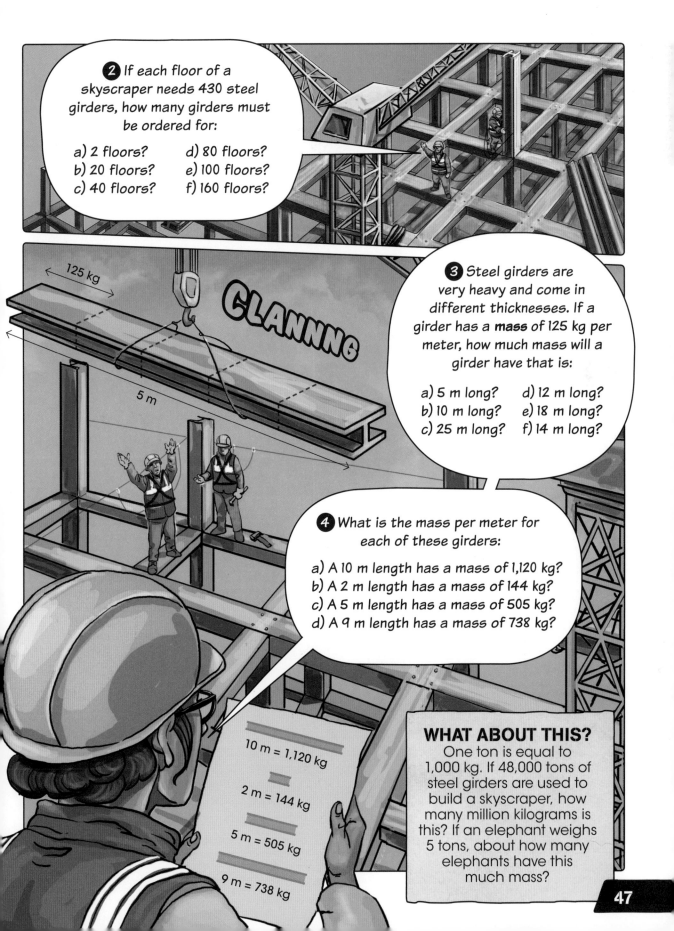

2 If each floor of a skyscraper needs 430 steel girders, how many girders must be ordered for:

a) 2 floors?
b) 20 floors?
c) 40 floors?
d) 80 floors?
e) 100 floors?
f) 160 floors?

3 Steel girders are very heavy and come in different thicknesses. If a girder has a **mass** of 125 kg per meter, how much mass will a girder have that is:

a) 5 m long?
b) 10 m long?
c) 25 m long?
d) 12 m long?
e) 18 m long?
f) 14 m long?

4 What is the mass per meter for each of these girders:

a) A 10 m length has a mass of 1,120 kg?
b) A 2 m length has a mass of 144 kg?
c) A 5 m length has a mass of 505 kg?
d) A 9 m length has a mass of 738 kg?

WHAT ABOUT THIS?

One ton is equal to 1,000 kg. If 48,000 tons of steel girders are used to build a skyscraper, how many million kilograms is this? If an elephant weighs 5 tons, about how many elephants have this much mass?

SKYSCRAPER USES

Skyscrapers are often built to be offices, living accommodation, hotels, or a mixture of these.

You have been asked to include offices, hotel rooms, apartments, restaurants, and stores in your skyscraper.

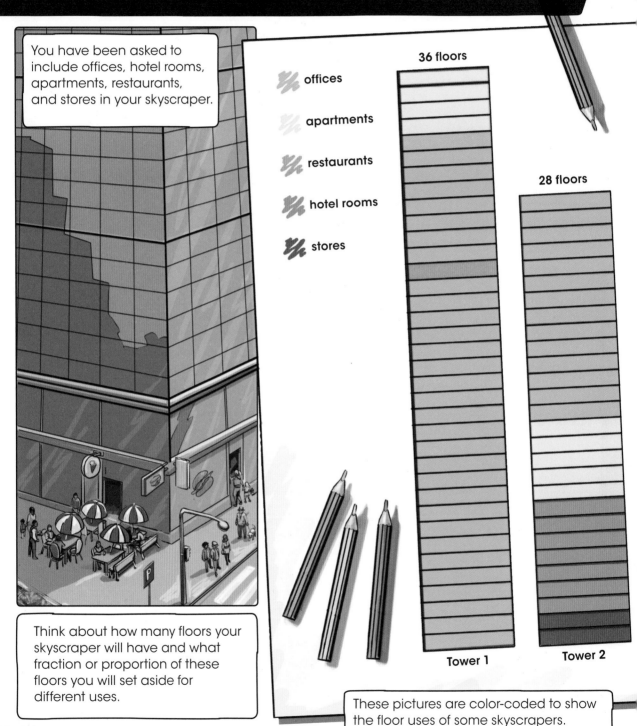

offices

apartments

restaurants

hotel rooms

stores

36 floors

28 floors

Tower 1

Tower 2

Think about how many floors your skyscraper will have and what fraction or proportion of these floors you will set aside for different uses.

These pictures are color-coded to show the floor uses of some skyscrapers.

1 Giving your answer as a fraction, write what proportion of:

a) tower 4 is stores
b) tower 1 is restaurants
c) tower 2 is apartments
d) tower 3 is restaurants.

32 floors

30 floors

2 Giving each answer as a fraction in its simplest form, write what proportion of:

a) tower 2 is stores
b) tower 4 is hotel rooms
c) tower 1 is apartments
d) tower 2 is hotel rooms.

3 Work out the proportion of each tower that is offices and **simplify** each fraction if you can.

4 Find out the answer to these questions:

a) Which tower has one quarter of its floors as hotel rooms?
b) Which tower has one eighth of its floors as apartments?
c) Which tower has one tenth of its floors as restaurants?

Tower 3

Tower 4

WHAT ABOUT THIS?
"Exactly half of tower ___ is
_____."
Look at the diagrams and find two ways of completing this sentence.

BUILDING YOUR SKYSCRAPER

Your next job is to design the services, such as electrical wiring, telephone connections, heating, plumbing, and toilets, for your skyscraper. These go inside the tower and make it a comfortable place to live and work.

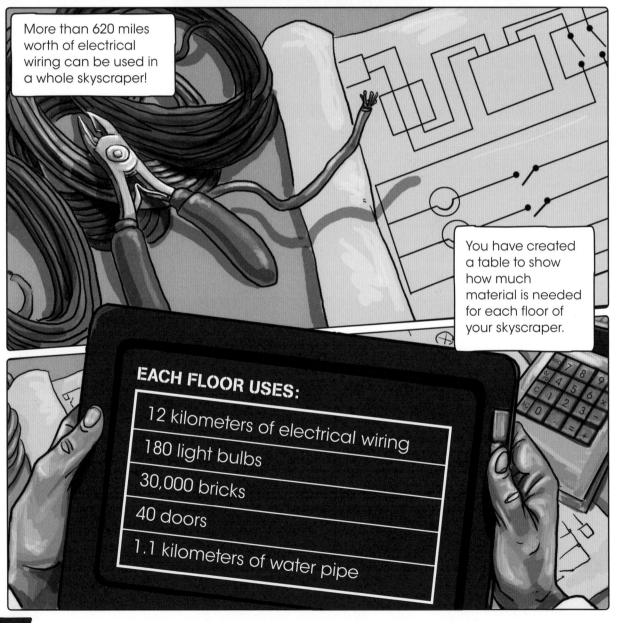

More than 620 miles worth of electrical wiring can be used in a whole skyscraper!

You have created a table to show how much material is needed for each floor of your skyscraper.

EACH FLOOR USES:

12 kilometers of electrical wiring
180 light bulbs
30,000 bricks
40 doors
1.1 kilometers of water pipe

SURVIVING EARTHQUAKES

The latest technology and math means that skyscrapers can be built taller and stronger than ever before.

Modern materials and building techniques will allow your tower to bend and twist to cope with the most extreme conditions, such as earthquakes and powerful winds.

This table shows the Richter Scale, which measures the seriousness of an earthquake using a scale of 1 (for the weakest) to 12 (for the strongest). The center of an earthquake is called the epicenter.

1	Usually not felt.
2	Felt only by sensitive people.
3	Vibrations similar to heavy traffic.
4	Rocking of objects.
5	Sleeping people are woken.
6	Damage to buildings within a few miles from the epicenter.
7	Serious damage up to 50 miles from the epicenter.
8	Great destruction, loss of life over several 100 miles from the epicenter.
9	Major damage and loss of life over 500 miles from the epicenter.
10	Many buildings are destroyed. There are some landslides.
11	Few buildings remain standing. Bridges and railways are destroyed.
12	Major or complete destruction.

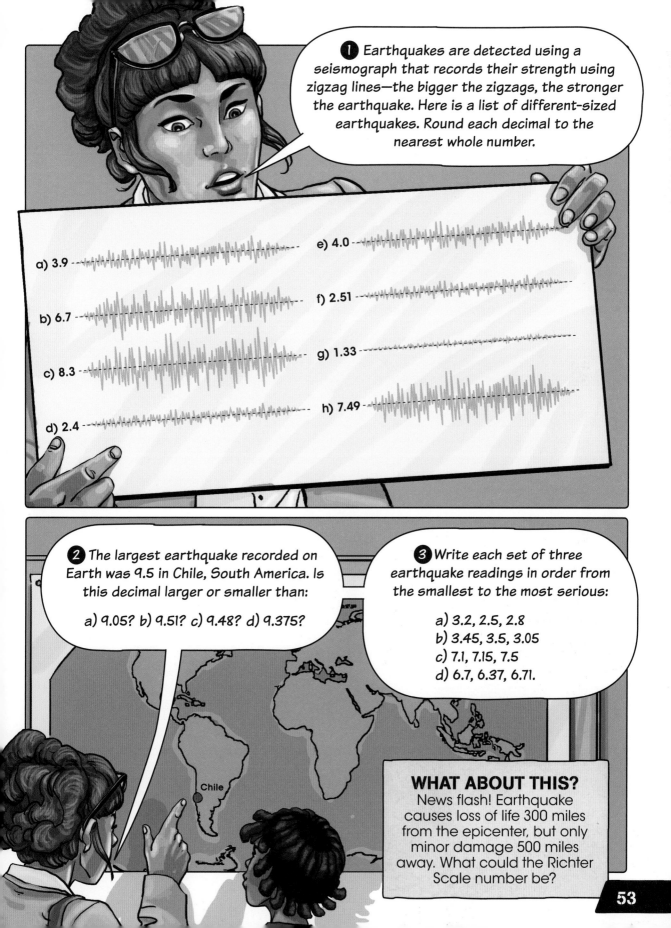

1 Earthquakes are detected using a seismograph that records their strength using zigzag lines—the bigger the zigzags, the stronger the earthquake. Here is a list of different-sized earthquakes. Round each decimal to the nearest whole number.

a) 3.9

b) 6.7

c) 8.3

d) 2.4

e) 4.0

f) 2.51

g) 1.33

h) 7.49

2 The largest earthquake recorded on Earth was 9.5 in Chile, South America. Is this decimal larger or smaller than:

a) 9.05? b) 9.51? c) 9.48? d) 9.375?

Chile

3 Write each set of three earthquake readings in order from the smallest to the most serious:

a) 3.2, 2.5, 2.8
b) 3.45, 3.5, 3.05
c) 7.1, 7.15, 7.5
d) 6.7, 6.37, 6.71.

WHAT ABOUT THIS?
News flash! Earthquake causes loss of life 300 miles from the epicenter, but only minor damage 500 miles away. What could the Richter Scale number be?

EMERGENCY STAIRS

Your skyscraper will need elevators, but it is also important to have staircases for emergencies.

In a staircase the "rise height" is the distance from the top of one stair to the top of the next, and the "tread depth" is the depth of the stair.

The recommended rise height is usually between 16 cm and 22 cm.

1. If the rise height for your staircase is 20 cm, what would be the height of a staircase with each of these numbers of stairs? Give your answers in meters.

a) 10 stairs b) 20 stairs c) 25 stairs.

2. Using your answers to question 1, find out how much shorter each staircase would be if the rise height for each stair was:

a) 18 cm b) 16 cm c) 12 cm.

20 cm

3. If the distance between the floors of a skyscraper is 3 meters and you put in 15 stairs for each floor, what would the rise height of each stair be?

3 m

140

139

138

137

4. A skyscraper has 140 floors, with 15 stairs for each floor. Each stair has a rise height of 19 cm.

a) How many stairs are there altogether?
b) What is the distance between each floor in centimeters?
c) What is the total height of the floors of this skyscraper in meters?

WHAT ABOUT THIS?
Measure the tread depth and rise height of some stairs. Can you work out the total height or total depth of the staircase?

GOING TO THE TOP

It is much faster to travel up and down in an elevator than to use the stairs. Some of the largest skyscrapers have more than 100 elevators for all the people moving around.

Your skyscraper will have express elevators that move very quickly, traveling at over 50 feet per second—that is faster than an Olympic sprinter!

Here are the speeds of the elevators in some of the world's tallest buildings.

NAME	AVERAGE SPEED OF ELEVATOR (FEET PER SECOND)
Empire State Building	20
Jin Mao Building	23
Burj Khalifa	26

Empire State Building

1 The highest an elevator will travel in the Empire State Building is 1,040 feet. How many seconds would the elevator take to go from ground level to the top, if going at the average speed and not stopping?

2 The highest an elevator will travel in the Burj Khalifa building is 1,664 feet. How many seconds will the elevator take to get there?

Burj Khalifa

3 The observation deck of the Jin Mao Building is 1,127 feet up and on the 88th floor.

a) How many seconds would the elevator take to reach there from ground level, going at an average speed?
b) If the elevator stops four times on its way to the 88th floor and each stop lasts 20 seconds, how long would the journey take? Give your answer in minutes and seconds.

Jin Mao Building

4 An elevator in a skyscraper took 3 minutes and 34 seconds to travel from ground level to the observation deck.

a) How many seconds is this?
b) If it left ground level at 12:25 and 40 seconds, what time did it reach the observation deck?

WHAT ABOUT THIS?
The Taipei 101 Tower has an elevator that can go at about 3,307 feet every minute. What is this in feet per second?

KEEPING IT CLEAN

The windows on your skyscraper are all in place
and the towering building itself looks impressive.

How are you going to keep all those windows clean? You're going to need some very brave window cleaners!

1 There are 110 floors on the Willis Tower in Chicago and each floor has 146 windows. How many windows are there altogether? Write the answer in figures and words.

2 The Burj Khalifa tower has 24,000 windows. The area of the glass is 120,000 m². What is the average area of each window?

3 Imagine stepping out to clean windows of the Burj Khalifa tower 800 meters above the ground! What fraction of a kilometer is 800 meters? Give your answer in its simplest form.

4 It takes a team of 36 window cleaners three months to clean the Burj Khalifa tower.

a) How long would you expect it to take 18 window cleaners to do the same job?
b) How many window cleaners might you need to do the same job in 1½ months?
c) How many window cleaners might you need to do the same job in one month?

WHAT ABOUT THIS?

Decide how many floors your skyscraper would have and how many windows for each floor on average. How many windows would this be in total? How long might they take to be cleaned?

>YOU+DO-THE÷MATH
LAUNCH A ROCKET INTO SPACE

ASTRONAUT SELECTION

You have been chosen to lead a mission into space and your first task is to select astronauts for your team. Choosing astronauts for space missions is difficult. Applicants must have the correct qualifications and experience.

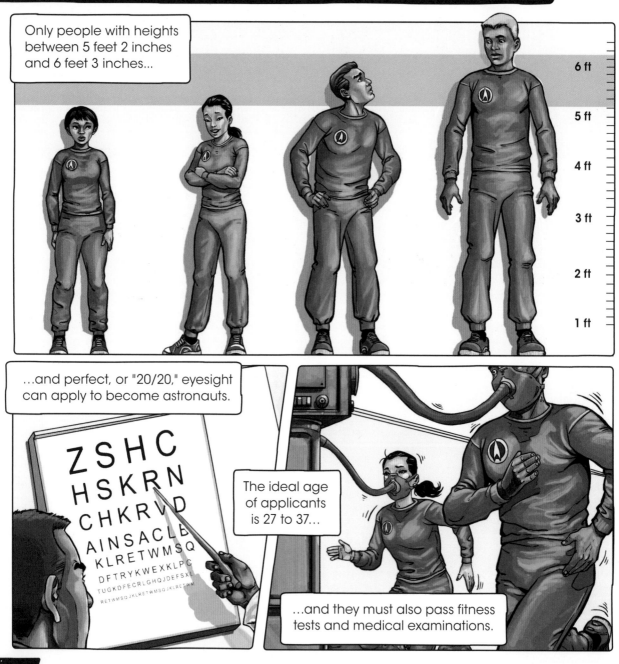

Only people with heights between 5 feet 2 inches and 6 feet 3 inches...

...and perfect, or "20/20," eyesight can apply to become astronauts.

The ideal age of applicants is 27 to 37...

...and they must also pass fitness tests and medical examinations.

ASTRONAUT CANDIDATES

NAME	GENDER	AGE	HEIGHT	EYESIGHT	✓/✗
Urvi Patel	Female	26	5 ft	20/20	
Brad Winchester	Male	30	5 ft 1 in	not 20/20	
Connor Wood	Male	28	5 ft 9 in	20/20	
Zoe Hurworth	Female	32	5 ft 4 in	20/20	✗
Samuel Wilkinson	Male	41	6 ft 4 in	20/20	
Kamelia Horacia	Female	37	5 ft 5 in	not 20/20	
Emily Smith	Female	39	5 ft 2 in	20/20	
Brendon Burke	Male	29	6 ft 2 in	20/20	
James Morton	Male	38	6 ft 10 in	20/20	

1 How many of the candidates are within the preferred age range?

2 Which of the candidates have the correct height to be an astronaut?

3 Three of the candidates have the correct height, the preferred age, and 20/20 eyesight. Who are they and are they male or female?

WHAT ABOUT THIS?
Find out your own height and see how much more you need to grow to be able to apply to be an astronaut. How much older do you need to be?

THE HISTORY OF ROCKETS

With your astronauts chosen, it's time to focus on the rocket.
But how much do you know about rockets?

This timeline shows some of the key events in the history of rockets.

Italian Claude Ruggieri launched animals inside rockets—the animals landed safely using parachutes.

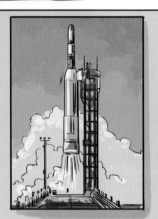

A Sputnik rocket launched the first artificial satellite, *Sputnik 1*.

An Atlas rocket launched *Mariner 2*, the first spacecraft to reach another planet.

1806   1926   1957   1961   1963

Robert Goddard invented and launched the first liquid-fueled rocket.

A Vostok-K rocket carried the first person into space, Russian cosmonaut Yuri Gagarin.

1. What happened 31 years before the year 2000?

2. Who invented and launched a rocket 70 years after 1856?

3. How many years after Apollo 11 landed on the Moon was the first Space Shuttle launched?

4. Which spacecraft reached another planet 41 years before SpaceShipOne reached space?

5. Which satellite went into space 56 years before the Olympic torch?

6. How long before the first Space Shuttle was launched was the first liquid-fueled rocket launched?

The United States launched the first Space Shuttle, *Columbia*.

The Russian Soyuz rocket took the Olympic torch to the International Space Station.

1969   1981   2004   2013   NOW

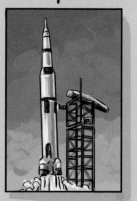

A Saturn V rocket launched Apollo 11, which took the first people to the Moon.

SpaceShipOne became the first privately developed reusable rocket craft to reach space.

Your mission into space!

WHAT ABOUT THIS?
Choose four events from the timeline and work out how many years ago each happened.

ROCKET SHAPES

Your rocket will need to be streamlined. A streamlined vehicle can move through the air easily. Rockets must be streamlined so that they can reach speeds fast enough to take them into space.

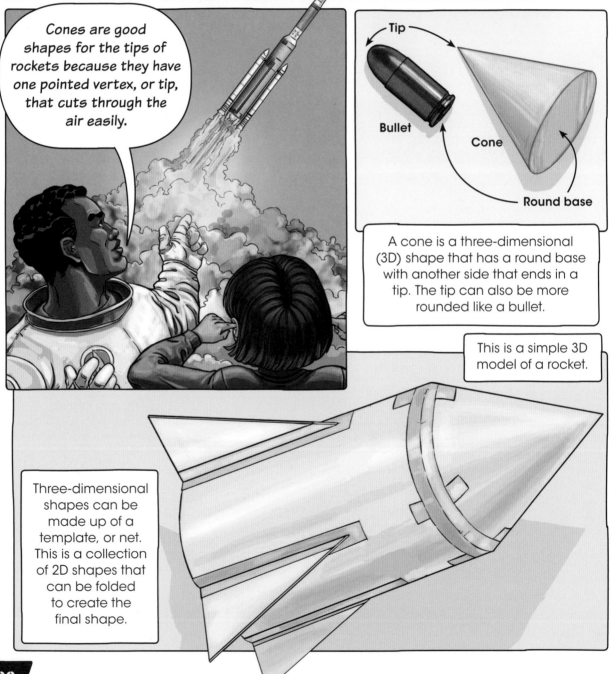

Cones are good shapes for the tips of rockets because they have one pointed vertex, or tip, that cuts through the air easily.

Tip

Bullet

Cone

Round base

A cone is a three-dimensional (3D) shape that has a round base with another side that ends in a tip. The tip can also be more rounded like a bullet.

This is a simple 3D model of a rocket.

Three-dimensional shapes can be made up of a template, or net. This is a collection of 2D shapes that can be folded to create the final shape.

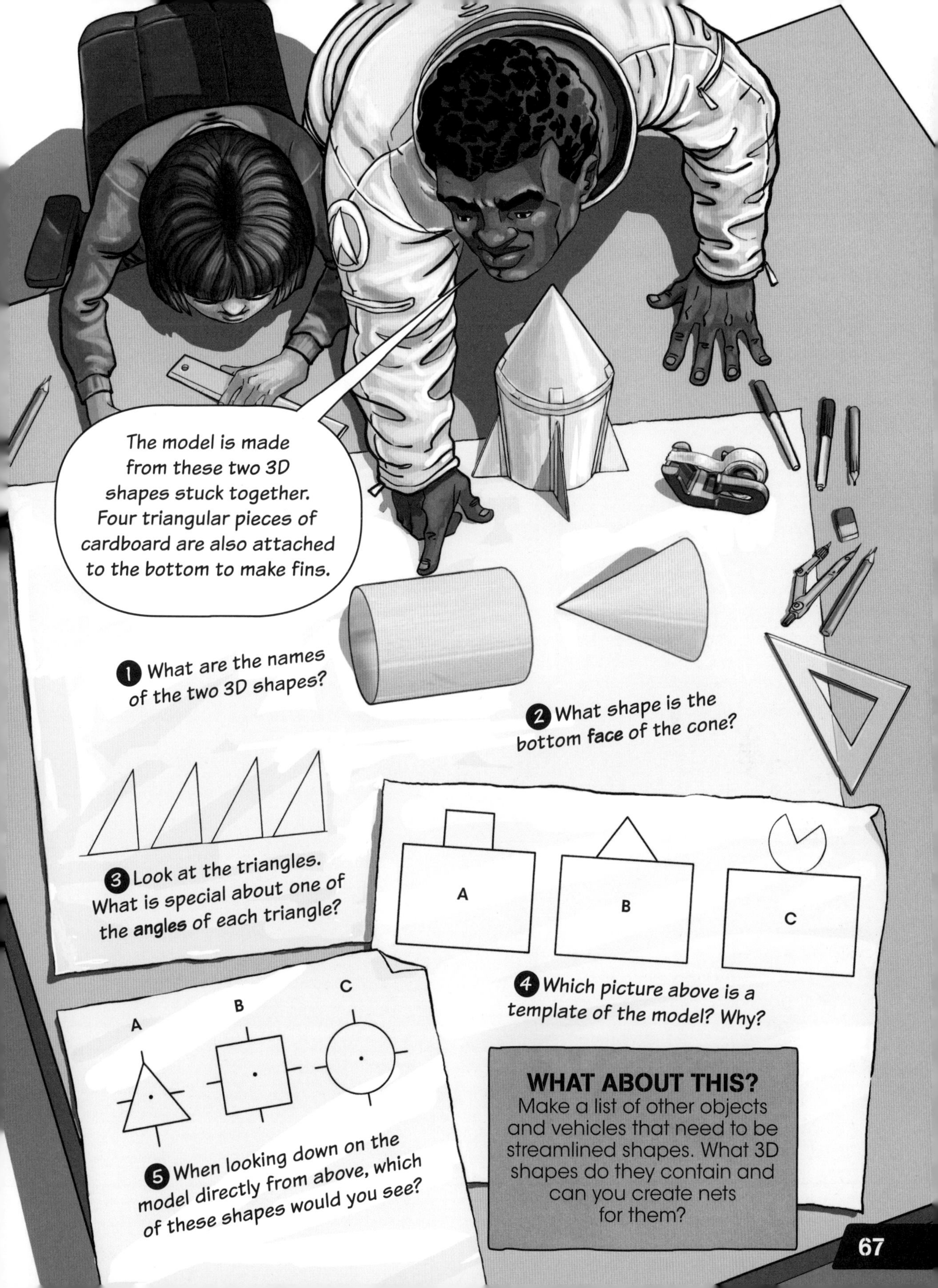

The model is made from these two 3D shapes stuck together. Four triangular pieces of cardboard are also attached to the bottom to make fins.

1 What are the names of the two 3D shapes?

2 What shape is the bottom **face** of the cone?

3 Look at the triangles. What is special about one of the **angles** of each triangle?

A   B   C

4 Which picture above is a template of the model? Why?

A   B   C

5 When looking down on the model directly from above, which of these shapes would you see?

WHAT ABOUT THIS?
Make a list of other objects and vehicles that need to be streamlined shapes. What 3D shapes do they contain and can you create nets for them?

THE SIZE OF ROCKETS

Rockets that carry spacecraft or satellites into space have to be really large. This is to hold all the fuel needed. Your next job is to look at other rockets to see how big yours needs to be.

Did you know that a space rocket can be taller than a 30-story building?

This table shows the heights of some famous buildings and rockets.

NAME	HEIGHT
Statue of Liberty (New York)	305 ft
Westminster Abbey (London)	226 ft
St. Paul's Cathedral (London)	364 ft
Arc de Triomphe (Paris)	164 ft
Atlas V rocket	190 ft
Ares 1 rocket	308 ft
Ariane V rocket	150 ft
N-1 rocket	344 ft
Saturn V rocket	364 ft

Atlas V rocket
190 ft

Ares 1 rocket
308 ft

Ariane V rocket
150 ft

N-1 rocket
344 ft

Saturn V rocket
364 ft

1 How much taller is:
a) the Atlas V rocket than the Arc de Triomphe?
b) the Ares 1 rocket than Westminster Abbey?
c) the Saturn V rocket than the Statue of Liberty?

2 List the five rockets in order of height from shortest to tallest.

3 Which rocket is:
a) the same height as St. Paul's Cathedral?
b) 39 feet taller than the Statue of Liberty?
c) 76 feet shorter than Westminster Abbey?

4 Round the height of each building and rocket to the nearest 10 feet.

WHAT ABOUT THIS?
Find out the height of other tall buildings in your country and see how much taller they are than the rockets listed here.

69

ROCKET CONSTRUCTION

A space rocket is built in several parts, called stages. Each stage has its own fuel and rocket engine. Your rocket will need three stages to carry it to outer space.

As the fuel in each stage is burned up, the stage comes off and falls back to Earth.

Here, stages 1, 2, and 3 drop off leaving only the upper stage to travel into space.

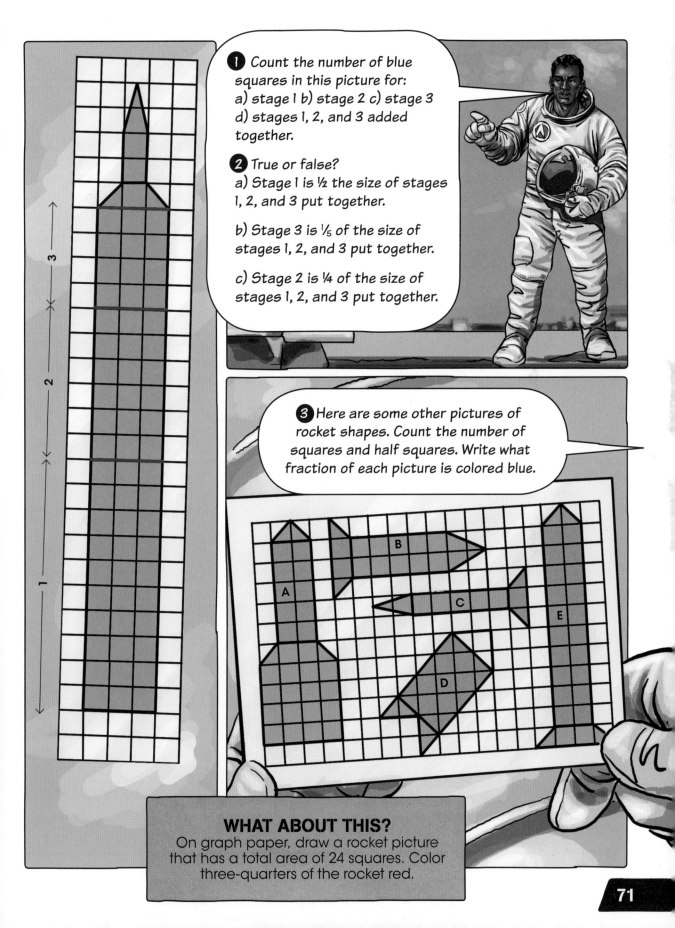

1 Count the number of blue squares in this picture for:
a) stage 1 b) stage 2 c) stage 3
d) stages 1, 2, and 3 added together.

2 True or false?
a) Stage 1 is ½ the size of stages 1, 2, and 3 put together.

b) Stage 3 is ⅛ of the size of stages 1, 2, and 3 put together.

c) Stage 2 is ¼ of the size of stages 1, 2, and 3 put together.

3 Here are some other pictures of rocket shapes. Count the number of squares and half squares. Write what fraction of each picture is colored blue.

WHAT ABOUT THIS?
On graph paper, draw a rocket picture that has a total area of 24 squares. Color three-quarters of the rocket red.

GETTING READY FOR LAUNCH

You can wear normal clothes inside the spacecraft because the air pressure is kept the same as on Earth.

If you go outside, however, you will have to wear a white pressurized space suit, because there is no air in space.

During launch, you will wear a special orange suit called an Advanced Crew Escape Suit, which will help protect you if there is an emergency.

420 newtons

1,270 newtons

Scientists measure the weight of things in units called newtons. An orange escape suit weighs 420 newtons on Earth and the white space suit weighs 1,270 newtons.

1 How much heavier is the space suit than the escape suit?

2 What is the total weight of the two types of space suit?

3 The total weight of an astronaut wearing an orange escape suit is 1,210 newtons. How much does the astronaut weigh?

4 What would each of these weigh on the Moon, if their weight on Earth is:

a) 2,000 newtons?
b) 2,050 newtons?
c) 1,950 newtons?

On the Moon, a person's weight is about one-fifth of their weight on Earth.

WHAT ABOUT THIS?
Find out your own weight and work out about how much you would weigh on the Moon. What if you were wearing a space suit too?

FOOD PREPARATION

When you go into space, you will need to eat and drink, just like you do on Earth.

Sometimes, food is kept in small plastic packets to stop crumbs getting into electronics.

The energy that you get from food is measured in units called calories. Here is the calorie content for different types of food.

	FOOD	CALORIES
	1 egg	78
	1 tortilla (flat bread)	101
	1 cheese slice	69
	1 apple	84
	1 slice of pizza	237
	1 serving of mashed potato	214
	1 dried apricot	16
	1 floret of broccoli	11
	1 cooked chicken breast	358

Bread is not usually taken because without gravity the crumbs might float around and cause problems with the equipment. Tortillas are taken instead.

1 Work out the total number of calories for:

a) two eggs
b) a tortilla and an egg
c) five dried apricots
d) three apples
e) a chicken breast and a serving of mashed potato
f) four florets of broccoli
g) a slice of pizza with an extra cheese slice on top
h) three slices of pizza.

2 Work out which items from the list were eaten if an astronaut ate:

a) two items with a total of 248 calories
b) three items with a total of 583 calories
c) three items with a total of 254 calories.

WHAT ABOUT YOU?
If you had to eat between 1,000 and 2,000 calories per day, which of the items and how many of them would you eat?

COUNTDOWN!

All your preparations are complete, so it's time for the countdown to your mission to begin.

A countdown is a list of all the things that have to be done before a rocket is launched.

It tells everyone, including the astronauts and the people in the control room, when each thing needs to be done.

Here is the countdown to your launch.

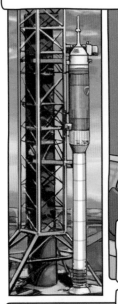

Step 1	-12 h 00 m 00 s	Final countdown begins
Step 2	-8 h 00 m 00 s	Check all electrics
Step 3	-1 h 30 m 00 s	Check launch system
Step 4	-8 m 00 s	Send "All systems go" message
Step 5	-4 m 00 s	Pressurize tanks
Step 6	-1 m 00 s	Switch to onboard power mode
Step 7	-10 s	Begin 10 second countdown
Step 8	00 s	Ignite main engine and LAUNCH!

BLAST OFF!

With the countdown complete, your rocket blasts clear of the launchpad.

During the first part of the flight, your rocket goes straight up, vertically.

It then begins to lean, gradually, until it is at the best angle for building up speed and getting into orbit around Earth.

Different steps of the launch.

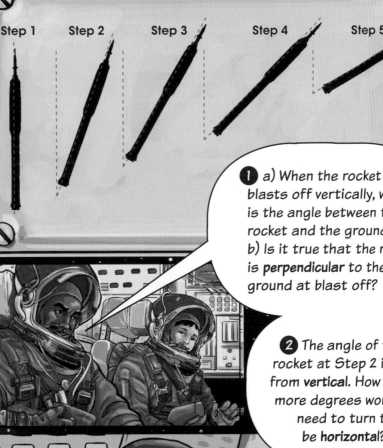

Step 1   Step 2   Step 3   Step 4   Step 5

1 a) When the rocket blasts off vertically, what is the angle between the rocket and the ground?
b) Is it true that the rocket is **perpendicular** to the ground at blast off?

2 The angle of the rocket at Step 2 is 20° from **vertical**. How many more degrees would it need to turn to be **horizontal**?

3 Use a protractor to measure the angles the rocket has leaned over at Steps 3, 4, and 5.

5 Is the angle at Step 5 an **acute** (less than 90°), an **obtuse** (greater than 90°) or a **reflex** angle (greater than 180°)?

4 At which step has the rocket turned through half a right angle?

6 At Step 5, how many more degrees would the rocket need to turn to be horizontal?

WHAT ABOUT THIS?
If a rocket is launched at 8:00 and reaches an angle of 70° to the vertical at 8:10, what is the average amount of turn per minute of the rocket?

INTO SPACE

As your rocket accelerates through Earth's atmosphere, the temperature outside your spacecraft drops.

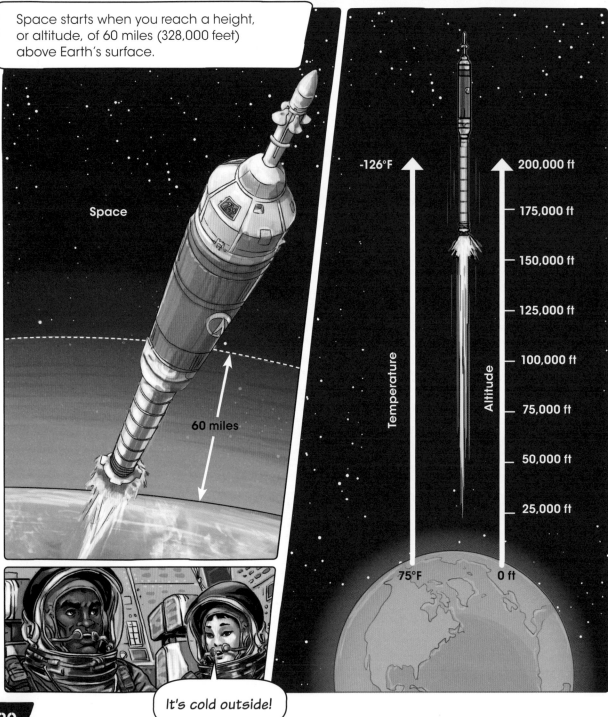

Space starts when you reach a height, or altitude, of 60 miles (328,000 feet) above Earth's surface.

Space

60 miles

-126°F

Temperature

Altitude

200,000 ft

175,000 ft

150,000 ft

125,000 ft

100,000 ft

75,000 ft

50,000 ft

25,000 ft

75°F

0 ft

It's cold outside!

This table shows the altitude of the rocket and the temperature at that height.

Altitude	Temperature	Altitude	Temperature
0 ft	75°F	14,000 ft	1°F
3,200 ft	48°F	16,400 ft	-4°F
6,400 ft	32°F	26,400 ft	-49°F
7,125 ft	25°F	33,000 ft	-76°F
11,300 ft	14°F	262,500 ft	-126°F

1 How many feet above Earth is the rocket when the temperature is:

a) -4°F?
b) -76°F?
c) -126°F?

2 When the rocket is at these heights, what is the **difference** in temperatures?

a) 3,200 ft and 0 ft
b) 6,400 ft and 0 ft
c) 7,125 ft and 6,400 ft
d) 26,400 ft and 6,400 ft
e) 7,125 ft and 14,000 ft
f) 33,000 ft and 262,500 ft.

3 At what height is the rocket when it is 63 degrees colder than the temperature at 11,300 ft?

4 At what height is the rocket when it is 45 degrees colder than its temperature at 16,400 ft?

WHAT ABOUT THIS?
Check the weather forecast to see what the temperature will be tomorrow. How much warmer will it be than the temperature at an altitude of 262,500 ft?

IN THE COCKPIT

Sitting in the pilot's seat of your spacecraft, you'll face a control panel that has lots of scales, dials, and readouts. These show information on how the rocket is performing.

Information can be presented in a wide range of displays and readouts. You need to be able to read this information quickly.

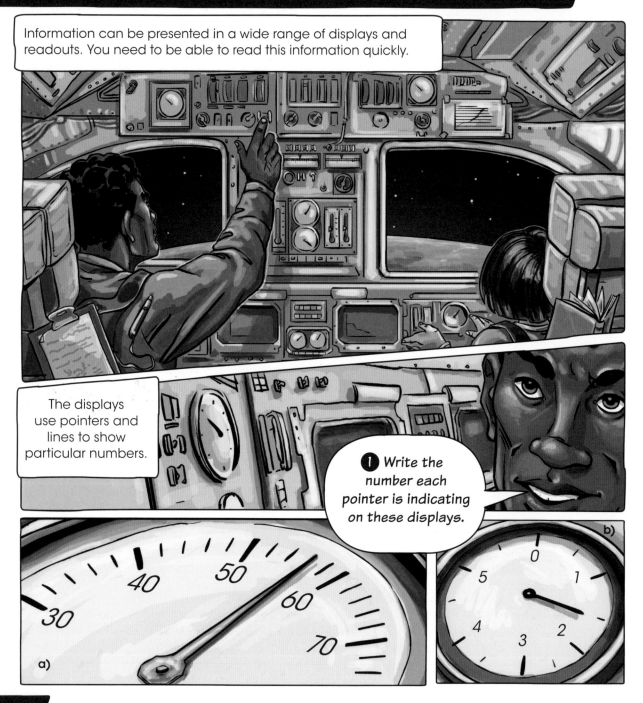

The displays use pointers and lines to show particular numbers.

1 Write the number each pointer is indicating on these displays.

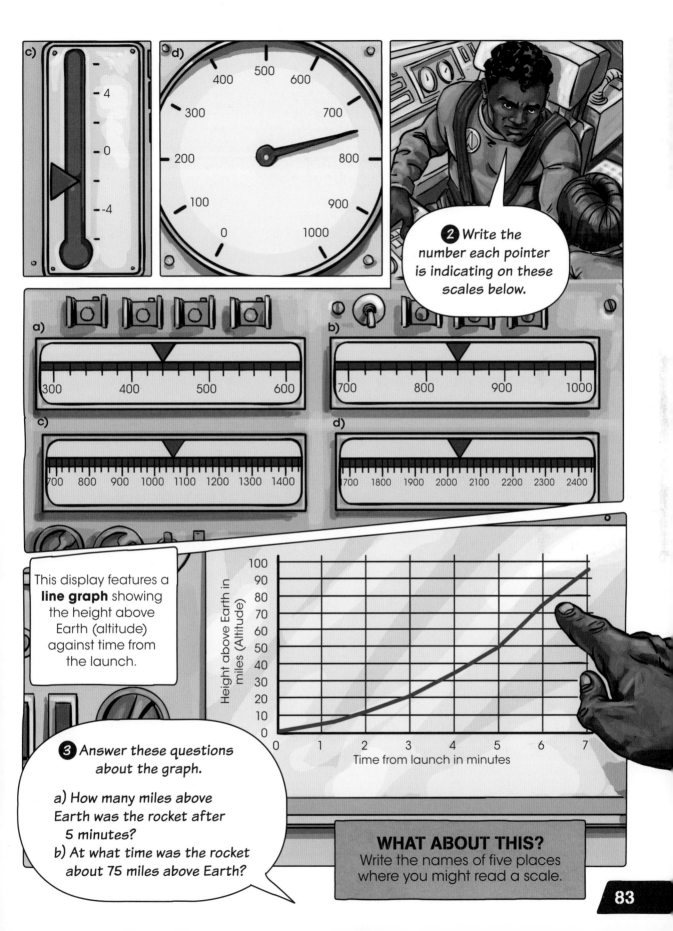

c)

d)

400 500 600
300   700
200   800
100   900
0   1000

2 Write the number each pointer is indicating on these scales below.

a)

300   400   500   600

b)

700   800   900   1000

c)

700 800 900 1000 1100 1200 1300 1400

d)

700 1800 1900 2000 2100 2200 2300 2400

This display features a **line graph** showing the height above Earth (altitude) against time from the launch.

Height above Earth in miles (Altitude)

100
90
80
70
60
50
40
30
20
10
0
   0   1   2   3   4   5   6   7
   Time from launch in minutes

3 Answer these questions about the graph.

a) How many miles above Earth was the rocket after 5 minutes?
b) At what time was the rocket about 75 miles above Earth?

WHAT ABOUT THIS?
Write the names of five places where you might read a scale.

83

IN ORBIT

The rocket has done its job in launching your spacecraft into orbit around Earth.

Your spacecraft orbits Earth every 1½ hours.

Earth

1½ hours

During each orbit, you will have 45 minutes of daylight and then 45 minutes of darkness.

These clocks show some of the sunrise and sunset times.

1 Write each time in words.

a)
Sunrise

b)
Sunrise

c)
Sunrise

d)
Sunset

e)
Sunset

f)
Sunset

RETURN TO EARTH

With your mission complete, your spacecraft can return to Earth. It has to re-enter the atmosphere before landing.

First, your spacecraft fires small rockets to slow down and turn around so that it descends bottom-first.

When it enters the atmosphere it gets very hot, so your craft needs heat shields to protect it.

As it gets closer to the ground, it slows down by making S-shaped turns, using parachutes, or by firing more rockets until it can land safely.

❶ Describe the series of turns shown in these pictures, using the words "quarter turn," "half turn," "clockwise," and "counterclockwise."

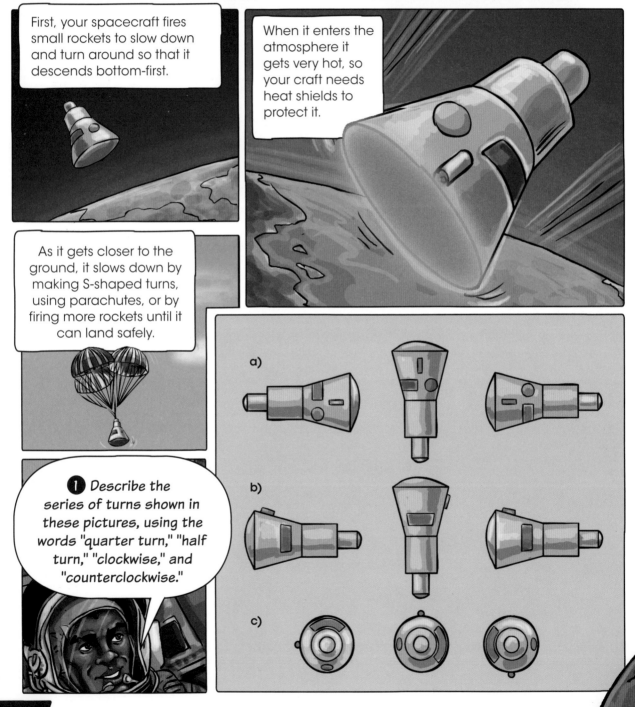

a)

b)

c)

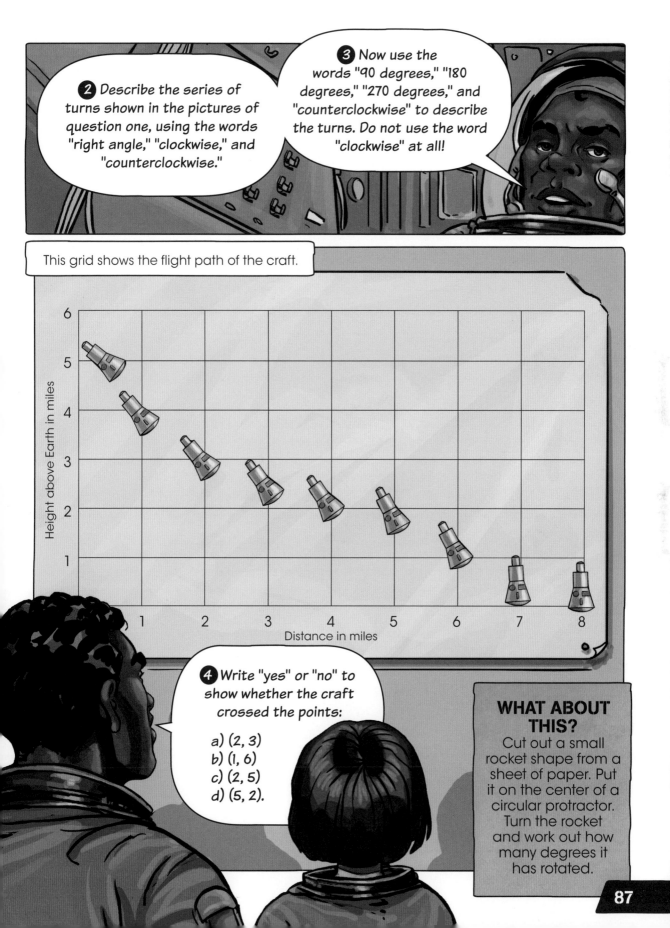

HIGH SPEEDS

Jet fighters are fast, small, and very maneuverable. They are used in many different roles, including air-to-air combat.

You have been given command of a squadron of jet fighters and their pilots.

Jet fighters are powered by jet engines. These work by air being sucked into the engine, compressed (squashed into a smaller volume), mixed with fuel, and then burned.

Blast of hot gases

Air sucked in

Burning fuel creates a powerful blast of hot gases, which rush out of the back of the engine, pushing the aircraft forward.

Most jet fighters go faster than the speed of sound—which is about 760 miles per hour (mph) at sea level. Speeds faster than sound are known as supersonic speeds.

The speed of sound gets slower as the jet fighters climb higher up into the atmosphere.

1 How much faster than the speed of sound is a jet fighter going when it is at:

a) 820 mph? b) 950 mph?
c) 990 mph? d) 1,010 mph?
e) 1,300 mph? f) 1,560 mph?

2 If a jet fighter is flying at the speed of sound this is known as Mach 1 (pronounced 'Mock one'). If it is flying twice the speed of sound, this is known as Mach 2. What speed is Mach 2?

3 If a car is driving at 19 mph, how many times faster than 19 mph is:
a) Mach 1?
b) Mach 2?

4 Work out these speeds:

a) Mach 1·1 is 75 mph faster than Mach 1. What speed is Mach 1·1?
b) Mach 1·2 is 150 mph faster than Mach 1. What speed is Mach 1·2?
c) Mach 1·9 is 75 mph slower than Mach 2. What speed is Mach 1·9?
d) Mach 1·5 is halfway between Mach 1 and Mach 2. What speed is Mach 1·5?

WHAT ABOUT THIS?
Find out the speeds of some other vehicles and see how they compare to a supersonic jet fighter.

DIFFERENT TYPES OF JET FIGHTER

The jet fighter you will fly is called the F-22 Raptor.
The letter "F" in its name stands for "fighter."

During your flight missions, you might come up against fighters from other air forces. Look at the data in this table to compare some of these jet fighters to your own.

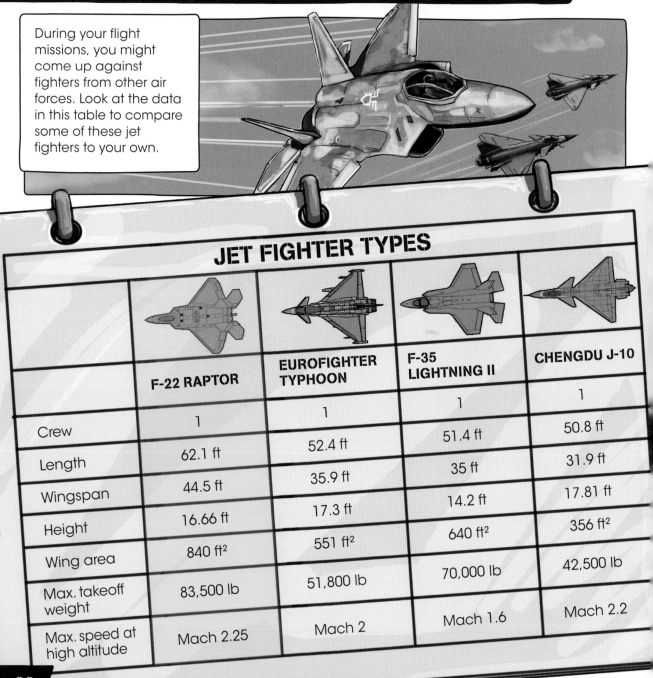

JET FIGHTER TYPES

	F-22 RAPTOR	EUROFIGHTER TYPHOON	F-35 LIGHTNING II	CHENGDU J-10
Crew	1	1	1	1
Length	62.1 ft	52.4 ft	51.4 ft	50.8 ft
Wingspan	44.5 ft	35.9 ft	35 ft	31.9 ft
Height	16.66 ft	17.3 ft	14.2 ft	17.81 ft
Wing area	840 ft²	551 ft²	640 ft²	356 ft²
Max. takeoff weight	83,500 lb	51,800 lb	70,000 lb	42,500 lb
Max. speed at high altitude	Mach 2.25	Mach 2	Mach 1.6	Mach 2.2

THE HISTORY OF JET FIGHTERS

Part of your training involves learning about the history of jet fighters and their use in combat.

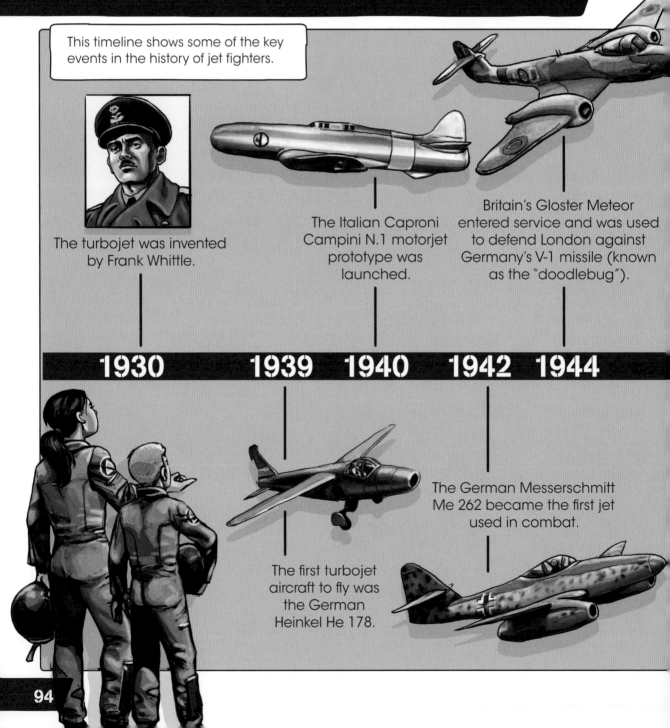

This timeline shows some of the key events in the history of jet fighters.

The turbojet was invented by Frank Whittle.

The Italian Caproni Campini N.1 motorjet prototype was launched.

Britain's Gloster Meteor entered service and was used to defend London against Germany's V-1 missile (known as the "doodlebug").

1930   1939   1940   1942   1944

The German Messerschmitt Me 262 became the first jet used in combat.

The first turbojet aircraft to fly was the German Heinkel He 178.

1. What happened 24 years before the year 1954?

2. Which fighter entered service 16 years after 1939?

3. How many years after the first flight of the Heinkel He 178 did the MiG-19 enter service?

4. How many years after the first turbojet aircraft were launched did the Eurofighter Typhoon enter service?

5. Which fighter entered service 51 years after the Hawker Hunter?

6. How long before the maiden flight of the Chengdu J-20 did the Gloster Meteor enter service?

The Chinese Chengdu J-20 made its first flight.

The British single-seat jet fighter, the Hawker Hunter, entered service.

The Eurofighter Typhoon entered service.

1950   1954 1955   2003 2005 2011

The first jet-to-jet dogfight in history occurred over Korea.

The Russian MiG-19 entered service.

The F-22 Raptor entered service.

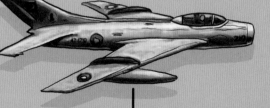

WHAT ABOUT THIS?
Choose four events from the timeline and work out how many years ago they happened.

JET FIGHTER USES

Every mission you fly will be different! One day you could be involved in air-to-air combat and the next you could be carrying out a vital role escorting other aircraft.

Depending on the mission, a jet fighter could be used for tasks such as reconnaissance (finding out what the enemy is doing)…

…attacking targets on the ground…

…air support for ground troops…

…or escorting other aircraft.

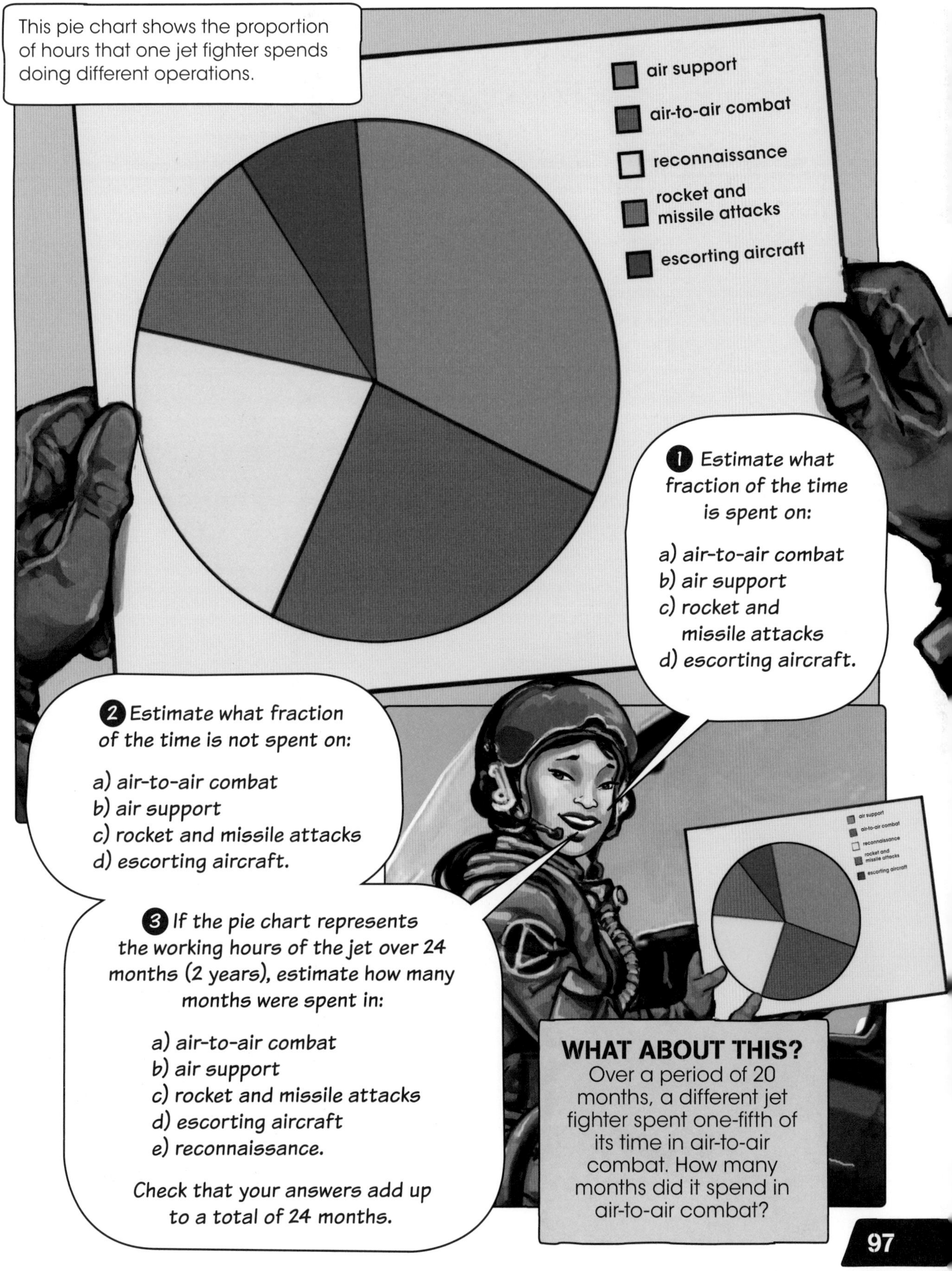

This pie chart shows the proportion of hours that one jet fighter spends doing different operations.

- air support
- air-to-air combat
- reconnaissance
- rocket and missile attacks
- escorting aircraft

1 Estimate what fraction of the time is spent on:

a) air-to-air combat
b) air support
c) rocket and missile attacks
d) escorting aircraft.

2 Estimate what fraction of the time is not spent on:

a) air-to-air combat
b) air support
c) rocket and missile attacks
d) escorting aircraft.

3 If the pie chart represents the working hours of the jet over 24 months (2 years), estimate how many months were spent in:

a) air-to-air combat
b) air support
c) rocket and missile attacks
d) escorting aircraft
e) reconnaissance.

Check that your answers add up to a total of 24 months.

WHAT ABOUT THIS?
Over a period of 20 months, a different jet fighter spent one-fifth of its time in air-to-air combat. How many months did it spend in air-to-air combat?

FIGHTER PILOT SELECTION PROCESS

Now you've learned the basics about your aircraft, it's time to choose the other pilots who will make up your squadron.

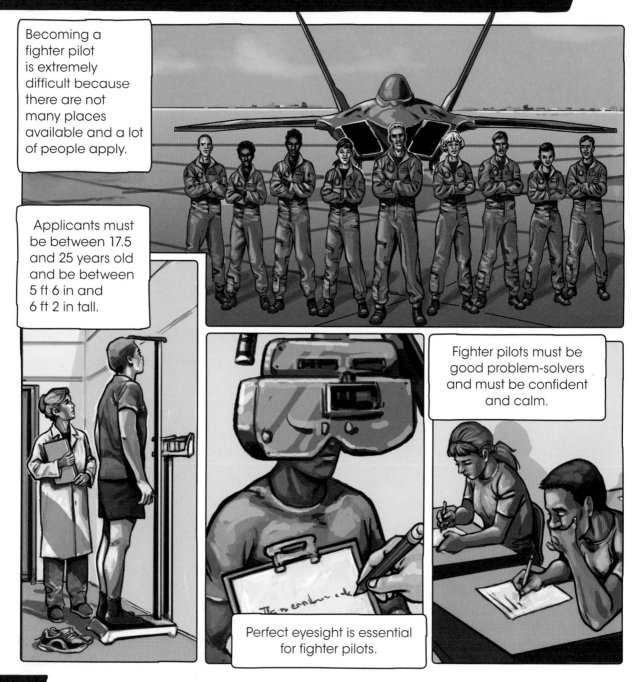

Becoming a fighter pilot is extremely difficult because there are not many places available and a lot of people apply.

Applicants must be between 17.5 and 25 years old and be between 5 ft 6 in and 6 ft 2 in tall.

Fighter pilots must be good problem-solvers and must be confident and calm.

Perfect eyesight is essential for fighter pilots.

The table below shows nine people who would like to apply for the pilot selection process.

1 How many of the candidates are within the correct age range to become a fighter pilot?

2 Which of the candidates are the correct height to become a fighter pilot?

FIGHTER PILOT CANDIDATES

NAME	M/F	AGE	HEIGHT	EYESIGHT
Luke Sharp	Male	19	5 ft 2 in	perfect
Ben Sherman	Male	16	5 ft 5 in	not perfect
Theo Wood	Male	24	5 ft 9 in	perfect
Emily Connor	Female	25	5 ft 8 in	perfect
Poppy Papadopoulou	Female	28	6 ft 3 in	perfect
Deepa Gorasia	Female	20	5 ft 10 in	not perfect
Simon Davis	Male	36	6 ft 0 in	perfect
Julia Hoffmann	Female	29	6 ft 1 in	perfect
Devon Richardson	Male	22	5 ft 6 in	perfect

3 Three of the candidates have the correct height, the preferred age, and perfect eyesight. Who are they and are they male or female?

WHAT ABOUT THIS?
Find out your own height and see how many more inches you need to grow to be able to apply to be a fighter pilot. How much older do you need to be?

FIGHTER PILOT TRAINING

With your squadron selected, it's time to climb into the cockpit and start your training.

Trainee pilots start by learning about flying regulations, navigation, and the weather. They also learn how aircraft work.

They will learn how to fly on flight simulators and training aircraft, before moving onto jet fighters.

The training is very tiring with 12-hour days. This is to ensure that pilots learn to cope with stressful situations.

A TYPICAL DAY IN PILOT TRAINING

06:00	Studying flight regulations
07:00	Physical training
09:00	Morning briefing
09:30	Emergency procedures test
10:15	Studying weather conditions
10:45	Flight schedule planning
12:00	Meal time
12:30	Simulated flight practice
15:55	Flight grading
16:40	Daily written exam
18:00	Rest and private study time

1 Write the time (using the words 'o'clock', 'past', or 'to') that a pilot starts:

a) Physical training
b) Emergency procedures test
c) Flight schedule planning
d) Flight grading
e) Daily written exam.

2 Write how many minutes there are from the start of each activity below, to the start of the activity the pilot must do next:

a) Morning briefing
b) Flight schedule planning
c) Flight grading
d) Daily written exam.

3 Write the activity that the pilot is doing at:

a)
b)
c)
d)
e)
f)

WHAT ABOUT THIS?
If a pilot trains for 12 hours each day, six days a week and for eight weeks, how many hours of training is this?

PILOT CALCULATIONS

While on a mission, you will have to make very quick calculations about a wide range of things.

These will include calculating the distance to other aircraft, including your target.

The information from your fighter's displays will also help you to work out how much fuel you have left and whether you need to **ascend** or **descend**.

You can use your fighter's speed to work out how long it will take to reach a target.

ROAR

You are flying at 5.8 miles above the ground, going at a speed of 310 mph.

The controller tells you to descend to 3.4 miles above the ground. You have also been advised to slow down to 220 mph.

1 How many miles must you descend?

2 By how many miles per hour must you slow down?

3 Once you reach 220 mph, you stay at this speed. How long would it take you to travel:

a) 220 mph? b) 110 mph? c) 55 mph?

4 If you are flying at 360 mph, how far would you travel in:

a) one minute?
b) two minutes?
c) three minutes?
d) five minutes?

5 a) How long would a 50-mile journey take flying at 500 mph?
b) How much longer would it take flying at 200 mph?

6 How much longer would a 90-mile journey take flying at 540 mph than at 900 mph?

WHAT ABOUT THIS?
If you know that your jet fighter is traveling at a speed of 12 miles per minute, what must you multiply by to work out the speed in miles per hour?

IN THE COCKPIT

When you're in the cockpit of a jet fighter, you need to be able to read all the dials and information displays.

Jet fighter pilots have to wear special helmets and face masks while flying.

These helmets are attached to cameras all the way around the aircraft—the pilots can even see an image of what's underneath their aircraft!

Some helmets also include night vision technology, so that pilots can "see" targets in the dark.

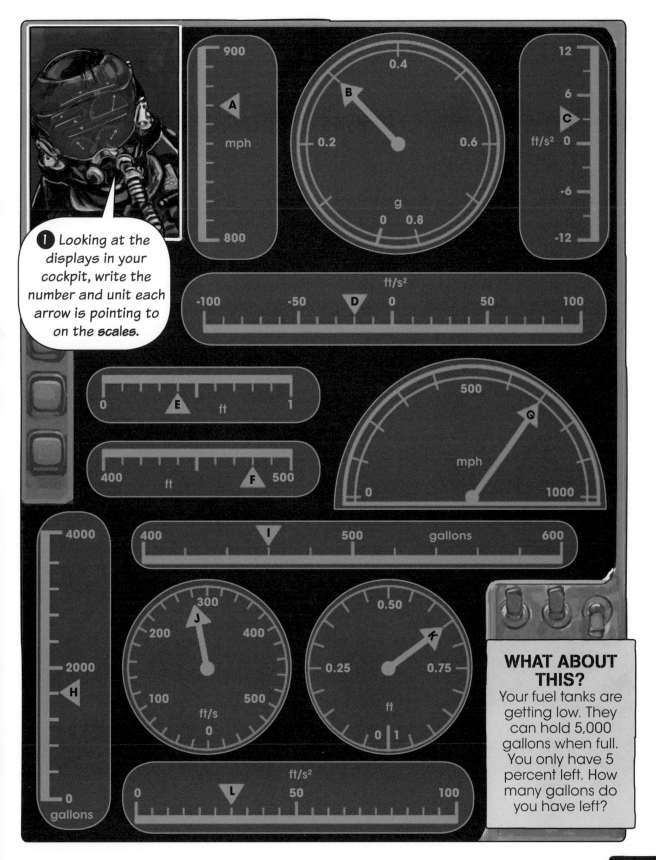

Looking at the displays in your cockpit, write the number and unit each arrow is pointing to on the scales.

WHAT ABOUT THIS?
Your fuel tanks are getting low. They can hold 5,000 gallons when full. You only have 5 percent left. How many gallons do you have left?

FORMATION FLYING

When flying with the rest of your squadron, you will have to fly close together in formation (organized patterns).

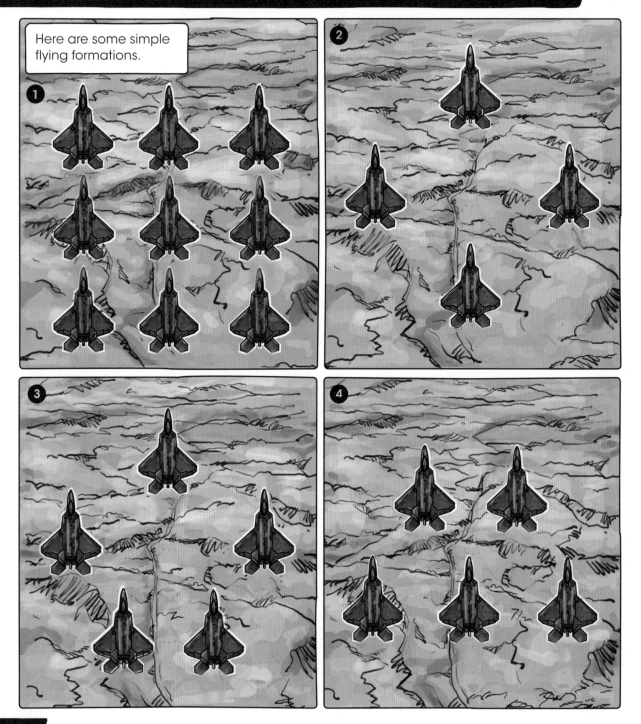

Here are some simple flying formations.

1 Write how many jets are in formation:

a) 1 b) 2 c) 3 d) 4.

2 Name the shapes made by the jets in formation:

a) 1 b) 2 c) 3 d) 4.

3 **Triangular numbers** are special numbers that can be arranged in a triangle. Each row in the triangle has one more than the row in front of it. Triangular numbers include 3, 6 and 10.

This picture shows six jets in a triangular formation. Row 2 has one more jet than row 1, and row 3 has one more jet than row 2.

a) Write out the first six triangular numbers.
b) Is it possible for 36 jets to fly in a triangular formation?

Row 1

Row 2

Row 3

WHAT ABOUT THIS?
Four jets fly in a square formation with the same number in each row and column. How many more jets are needed to make the next largest square formation?

G-FORCE

When performing aerobatic twists and turns in your jet fighter, you will experience high g-forces (gravitational forces).

G-forces pull on you and can make you feel heavier. You will have the same experience when riding a roller coaster.

WOOOSH!

1-g feels the same as the Earth's normal pull of gravity. 2-g makes you feel twice as heavy, 3-g makes you feel three times as heavy and so on. Pilots train to cope with g-forces inside a large machine called a centrifuge.

Making very sharp turns in a jet fighter can create g-forces of up to 12-g! High g-forces can damage the human body.

G-suits are worn by pilots to help protect them. These suits allow pilots to withstand more extreme maneuvers than they would without the suit.

G-suits are really helpful when making sharp turns or spinning upside-down.

Scientists use units called newtons (N) to measure weight.

1 For a pilot weighing 800 N, write how heavy he would feel at:

a) 2-g b) 3-g c) 4-g d) 5-g e) 6-g f) 7-g
g) 8-g h) 9-g i) 10-g j) 11-g k) 12-g.

2 A fighter pilot experiences 3-g during a maneuver. How heavy would she feel if she normally weighs:

a) 370 N? b) 430 N? c) 570 N? d) 680 N?

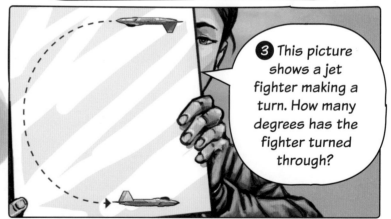

3 This picture shows a jet fighter making a turn. How many degrees has the fighter turned through?

WHAT ABOUT THIS?
It is possible to feel a g-force of zero, or 0-g, when you feel weightless. This can happen when a jet is in a dive. Find your own weight and see what you would weigh at 0-g, 1-g, 2-g, 3-g, 4-g and so on.

WEATHER DATA

A jet fighter pilot needs to understand weather conditions. Clouds can cause turbulence and if the wind is blowing strongly, it could blow you off course.

This **line graph** shows the strength and direction of the wind during one day.

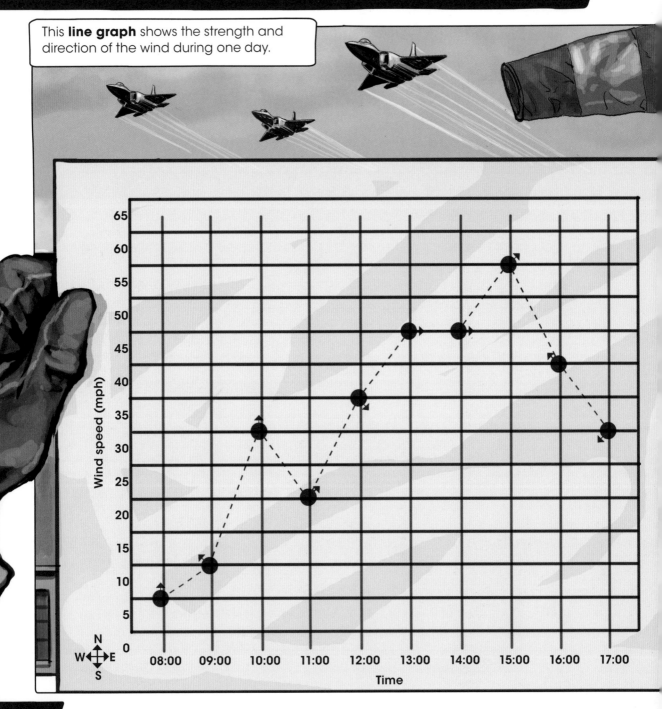

1 What is the speed of the wind at:

a) 09:00? b) 12:00? c) 14:00? d) 16:00? e) 09:30? f) 12:30?

2 At which time or times during the day is the wind:

a) 35 mph? b) 40 mph? c) 20 mph? d) 30 mph?

3 Write the direction the wind is going at each hour between 08:00 and 17:00.

4 At which time of day is the wind the strongest?

5 Jet fighter pilots must adjust their direction if there is a strong wind. This line shows the direction the pilot will fly to reach the target when the wind is from the north. What is the **angle** between the flight direction and the direction to the target in the picture below?

wind from north

flight direction

direction to the target

WHAT ABOUT THIS?
Look at today's weather forecast. What is the wind speed? What is the wind direction? How might you need to adjust your flying to take these into account?

RECONNAISSANCE

One of your tasks is to fly over enemy positions, taking photographs. This is known as a reconnaissance mission.

A jet fighter has cameras for taking pictures of the location.

A reconnaissance mission gathers information about a particular place. The aim could be to look for possible targets or find out the enemy's position.

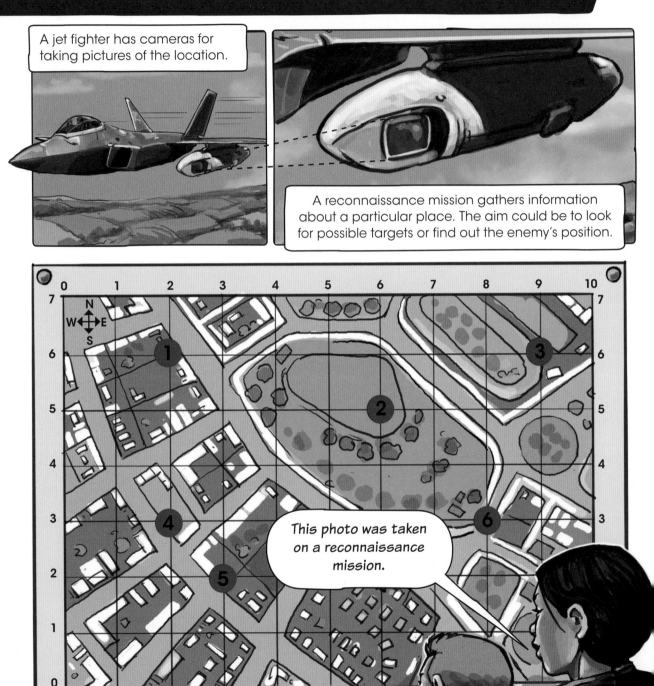

This photo was taken on a reconnaissance mission.

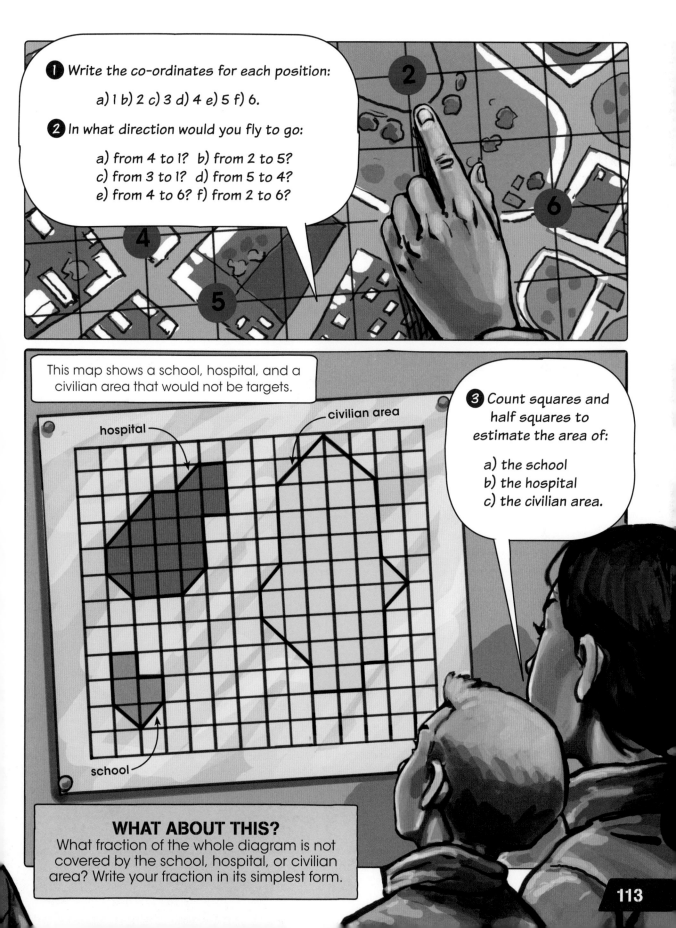

1 Write the co-ordinates for each position:

a) 1 b) 2 c) 3 d) 4 e) 5 f) 6.

2 In what direction would you fly to go:

a) from 4 to 1? b) from 2 to 5?
c) from 3 to 1? d) from 5 to 4?
e) from 4 to 6? f) from 2 to 6?

This map shows a school, hospital, and a civilian area that would not be targets.

3 Count squares and half squares to estimate the area of:

a) the school
b) the hospital
c) the civilian area.

hospital

civilian area

school

WHAT ABOUT THIS?
What fraction of the whole diagram is not covered by the school, hospital, or civilian area? Write your fraction in its simplest form.

AIR-TO-AIR COMBAT

When flying, your jet fighter can be turned in three different ways. These are known as roll, yaw, and pitch.

If a jet is flying forward in a straight line it can be rolled so one wing is lower than the other one.

Yaw means a turn which, when flying **horizontally**, turns the jet to point to a different compass direction.

Pitch is moving the jet so the front of the jet tilts up or down.

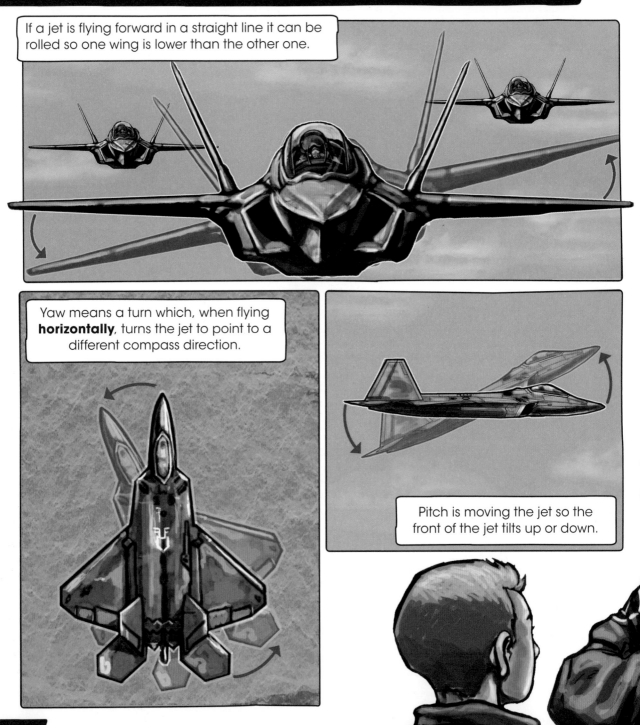

1 Describe the series of turns shown in these pictures, saying how many right angles or half-right angle turns are being made each time. Include the words "clockwise" and "counterclockwise" in your descriptions.

A.

B.

C.

2 Which of these pictures shows jet fighters flying on **parallel** flight-paths?

A.

B.

C.

D.

E.

WHAT ABOUT THIS?
Which of the jets in question 2 are flying horizontally? Which are flying **vertically**?

Congratulations! Your team has solved the crime and caught the criminal! Check your answers here to see how well you did.

PAGES 6–7

1. a) 8,000,000 b) ½, 0.5, 50%

2. 0.5, 50%; 0.1, 10%; 0.25, 25%; $^9/_{100}$, 0.09

3. 72,000

4. 4,860,000

WHAT ABOUT THIS? There were 1.6 million crimes against people and 6.4 million against property.

PAGES 8–9

1. a) Alice b) Alice c) Iain

2. a) 15 in b) 20 in

3. a) 17.5 b) 35

4. a) 23.3 b) 26.3 c) 32.3

WHAT ABOUT THIS? Dan, Alice, David and Paula all have a BMI between 18 and 30.

PAGES 10–11

1. a (2, 6) b (10, 6) c (13, 7) d (8, 5) e (5, 1) f (8, 1) g (9, 9) h (0, 9)

2. a) behind the right hand sofa b) on the oval table c) in or near the plant d) on the armchair

3. a) 160 in b) 80 in c) 180 in d) 60 in

WHAT ABOUT THIS? The perimeter would be 240 inches.

PAGES 12–13

1. a) 3 b) 18

2. a) 200 b) 90 c) 15

3. 305, but there are only 300 people in the concert hall

4. $^{13}/_{20}$ of 300 = 195, $^2/_3$ of 300 = 200. $^{13}/_{20}$ is a better estimate for the loops section.

PAGES 14–15

1. a) 11 b) $^{11}/_{36}$ c) $^3/_{36} = ^1/_{12}$

2. a) $^9/_{36} = ^1/_4$ b) $^{12}/_{36} = ^1/_3$ c) $^{11}/_{36}$

3. a) $^6/_{36} = ^1/_6$ b) $^4/_{36} = ^1/_9$ c) $^3/_{36} = ^1/_{12}$

4. a) $^{21}/_{36} = ^7/_{12}$ b) $^{20}/_{36} = ^5/_9$ c) $^{22}/_{36} = ^{11}/_{18}$

5. a) 0 b) 3 c) 1

WHAT ABOUT THIS? Suspect 3 was at the scene of the crime.

PAGES 16–17

1. a) ten past twelve b) five to one c) twenty-five past one

2. a) no b) yes c) no d) no e) yes f) no g) no h) yes

3. a) 35 minutes b) ¾ hour or 45 minutes
c) ½ hour or 30 minutes

*WHAT ABOUT THIS? Suspects 1 and 2 could
not have committed the crime, but suspect
3 could have done it.*

PAGES 18–19
1. 80 squares

2. a) 4 squares b) 9 squares c) 9 squares
d) 16 squares e) 2 squares

3. 40 squares

4. $^{40}/_{80} = ^1/_2$, 50%

5. a) 400 ft² b) 200 ft²

*WHAT ABOUT THIS? It took her 17 $^1/_2$ hours to
watch all of the camera footage.*

PAGES 20–21
1. a) two o'clock b) twenty to four
c) quarter to five d) twenty-five to seven

2. a) 15 minutes b) 70 minutes c) 35 minutes
d) 75 minutes

3. a) talking to victims b) securing the
perimeter c) talking to witnesses
d) collecting evidence

*WHAT ABOUT THIS? The detective has worked
for 10 hours in total.*

PAGES 22–23
1. Frequencies for men: 2, 6, 4, 2, 0, 0, 1
Frequencies for women: 4, 0, 2, 2, 3, 2, 0

2. a) 2 b) 0 c) 2 d) 6

3. a) 2 b) 0 c) 3 d) 4

4. 2

*WHAT ABOUT THIS? The suspects are a male
in his 30s with brown hair and a male in his
40s with brown hair.*

PAGES 24–25
1. a) 11 b) 8 c) 12 d) 4

2. No men in their 40s have a Master's
degree, but three men between the ages of
38 and 52 have a degree.

3. Sam Evans, Tom Collins, Toby Franks

4. Two have a college degree and one of those
has a car.

*WHAT ABOUT THIS? There are three suspects
with no education who own a car: Simon
Stone, James Jones, and Chris Carter.*

PAGES 26–27
1. a) A 3.8 cm, B 3.5 cm b) A 12 cm, B 11.4 cm
c) A 3 cm, B 2 cm d) A 7.3 cm, B 6.8 cm
e) A 2.8 cm, B 2.1 cm

2. A 4.7 cm, B 4.6 cm

3. 3:12 or 1:4

4. A 3.8:12, B 3.5:11.4

PAGES 28–29
1. a) $900 b) $6,300 c) $1,320 d) $770 e) $1,440
f) $1,680

2. a) $1,953 b) $381 c) $1,521

3. Simon Stone

*WHAT ABOUT THIS? $79 has not been paid
into the bank.*

PAGES 30–31
1. Answers may vary, e.g., go west along St.
James's Rd, turn left and head south down
Green Street.

2. 6

3. The suspect could be in the park or in the
department store. He is unlikely to be in the
police station!

4. 9

*WHAT ABOUT THIS? There are more than
20 different routes from M to P.*

DESIGN A SKYSCRAPER ANSWERS

Congratulations! You have built the world's tallest skyscraper! Check your answers here to see how well you did.

PAGES 34–35

1. a) 1 b) 0 c) 8 d) 8 e) 6 f) 0 g) 5

2. a) 2 b) 3 c) 6 d) 6 e) 5 f) 1 g) 5

3. a) cylinder, cone b) cuboid, cylinder, sphere c) square-based pyramid d) cuboid, square-based pyramid e) triangular prism

4. a) 2 b) 7 c) 4 d) 8 e) 4

5. 1 – e, 2 – c and d, 3 – b, 4 – a
   you wouldn't see 5

PAGES 36–37

1. a) 426 ft b) 131 ft c) 2,407 ft

2.

NAME	HEIGHT
Big Ben	315 ft
The Gherkin	591 ft
The Shard	1,017 ft
Empire State Building	1,250 ft
Jin Mao Building	1,381 ft
Petronas Twin Towers	1,482 ft
Taipei 101 Tower	1,670 ft
One World Trade Center	1,776 ft
Makkah Royal Clock Tower	1,972 ft
Shanghai Tower	2,073 ft
Burj Khalifa	2,722 ft

3. a) Shanghai Tower b) One World Trade Center c) The Shard

4.

NAME	HEIGHT TO NEAREST 100FT
Big Ben	300 ft
The Gherkin	600 ft
The Shard	1,000 ft
Empire State Building	1,300 ft
Jin Mao Building	1,400 ft
Petronas Twin Towers	1,500 ft
Taipei 101 Tower	1,700 ft
One World Trade Center	1,800 ft
Makkah Royal Clock Tower	2,000 ft
Shanghai Tower	2,100 ft
Burj Khalifa	2,700 ft

PAGES 38–39

1. a) 40 m b) 120 m c) 380 m d) 450 m

2. a) 1930s b) 380 m c) 130 m d) 70 m

3. 1990–2010

4. 2000–2010

WHAT ABOUT THIS? It was the tallest between 2000–2010. There is no mark because it had been overtaken by the end of the decade.

PAGES 40–41

1. a) Site C b) Site A c) Site C d) Site B

2. a) (5,1) b) (3,5) c) (3,5) d) (5,4)

3. south

4. north west

PAGES 42–43

1. a) 240 ft b) 240 ft c) 220 ft d) 320 ft

2. a) 28 squares b) 23 squares
   c) 28 squares d) 24 squares

3. No

4. a) 2,800ft² b) 2,300ft² c) 2,800ft² d) 2,400ft²

5. Yes, A and B have the same perimeters but different areas, while A and C have the same areas but different perimeters.

WHAT ABOUT THIS? The volume of the skyscraper is 12,500,000 m³.

PAGES 44–45

1. 8 ft below ground level (–8 ft)

2. a) –4 ft b) –5 ft c) –10 ft

3. a) –4 b) 1 c) –4 d) 11 e) –8 f) –7

4. a) 5 b) 7 c) 10

WHAT ABOUT THIS? There are 76 floors above ground level.

PAGES 46–47

1. A, B, C, D, E, K, M, O, U, V, W, X, Y

2. a) 860 b) 8,600 c) 17,200 d) 34,400
   e) 43,000 f) 68,800

3. a) 625 kg b) 1,250 kg c) 3,125 kg d) 1,500 kg
   e) 2,250 kg f) 1,750 kg

4. a) 112 kg b) 72 kg c) 101 kg d) 82 kg

WHAT ABOUT THIS? It is 48 million kg, which is equivalent to 9,600 elephants.

PAGES 48–49

1. a) $^1/_{30}$ b) $^1/_{36}$ c) $^5/_{28}$ d) $^3/_{32}$

2. a) $^1/_{14}$ b) $^1/_2$ c) $^1/_9$ d) $^1/_4$

3. 1 – $^{31}/_{36}$ 2 – $^1/_2$ 3 – $^{25}/_{32}$ 4 – $^{11}/_{30}$

4. a) 2 b) 3 c) 4

WHAT ABOUT THIS?
   Exactly half of tower 2 is offices.
   Exactly half of tower 4 is hotel rooms.

PAGES 50–51

1. a) 720 km b) 1,056 km c) 1,440 km

2. a) 9,000 b) 18,180 c) 27,000

3. a) 960,000 b) 2,100,000 c) 3,300,000

4. a) 1,600 b) 4,000 c) 6,000

5. a) 66 km b) 132 km c) 176 km

WHAT ABOUT THIS? 1,020 miles of telephone cable was used.

PAGES 52–53

1. a) 4 b) 7 c) 8 d) 2 e) 4 f) 3 g) 1 h) 7

2. a) larger b) smaller c) larger d) larger

3. a) 2.5, 2.8, 3.2 b) 3.05, 3.45, 3.5
   c) 7.1, 7.15, 7.5 d) 6.37, 6.7, 6.71

WHAT ABOUT THIS? The earthquake measured 8 on the Richter Scale.

PAGES 54–55

1. a) 2 m, b) 4 m, c) 5 m

2. a) 20 cm, 40 cm, 50 cm b) 40 cm, 80 cm, 100 cm c) 80 cm, 160 cm, 200 cm

3. 20 cm

4. a) 2,100 b) 285 cm c) 399 m

PAGES 56–57

1. 52 seconds

2. 64 seconds

3. a) 49 seconds b) 2 minutes 9 seconds

4. a) 214 seconds b) 12:29 and 14 seconds

WHAT ABOUT THIS? That is 55.1 feet per second.

PAGES 58–59

1. a) 16,060, sixteen thousand and sixty

2. a) 5 m²

3. a) $^4/_5$

4. a) 6 months b) 72 c) 108

Congratulations!
You have completed your space mission! Check your answers here to see how well you did.

PAGES 62–63

1. Five

2. Connor, Zoe, Kamelia, Emily, and Brendon

3. Connor, Zoe, and Brendon (male, female, and male)

PAGES 64–65

1. A Saturn V rocket launched Apollo 11.

2. Robert Goddard

3. 12 years

4. Mariner 2

5. Sputnik 1

6. 55 years

PAGES 66–67

1. Cone and tube (or cylinder)

2. Circle

3. One angle is a right angle.

4. C. The top part rolls up to make the cone.

5. C

PAGES 68–69

1. a) 26 feet b) 82 feet c) 59 feet

2. Ariane V, Atlas V, Ares 1, N-1, Saturn V

3. a) Saturn V b) N-1 c) Ariane V

4.

NAME	HEIGHT
Statue of Liberty (New York)	310 ft
Westminster Abbey (London)	230 ft
St. Paul's Cathedral (London)	360 ft
Arc de Triomphe (Paris)	160 ft
Atlas V rocket	190 ft
Ares 1 rocket	310 ft
Ariane V rocket	150 ft
N-1 rocket	340 ft
Saturn V rocket	360 ft

PAGES 70–71

1. a) 30 b) 18 c) 12 d) 60

2. a) true b) true c) false, it is $\frac{3}{5}$

3. a) 10 out of 30 squares = $\frac{1}{3}$
   b) 3 out of 15 squares = $\frac{1}{5}$
   c) 2 out of 8 squares = $\frac{1}{4}$
   d) 12 out of 14 squares = $\frac{6}{7}$
   e) 20 out of 24 squares = $\frac{5}{6}$

PAGES 72–73

1. 850 newtons

2. 1,690 newtons

3. 790 newtons

4. a) 400 newtons b) 410 newtons
   c) 390 newtons

PAGES 74–75

1. a) 156 calories   b) 179 calories,
   c) 80 calories   d) 252 calories,
   e) 572 calories   f) 44 calories,
   g) 306 calories   h) 711 calories

2. a) one slice of pizza and one floret of broccoli
   b) one chicken breast, one serving of mashed potato, and one floret of broccoli
   c) one tortilla, one cheese slice, and one apple

PAGES 76–77

1. a) 4 minutes b) 90 minutes
   c) 480 minutes

2. a) 60 seconds b) 240 seconds
   c) 480 seconds

3. Step 1 3:30 a.m., Step 2 7:30, Step 3 2:00, Step 4 3:22, Step 5 3:26, Step 6 3:29, Step 7 3:29 and 50 seconds

PAGES 78–79

1. a) 90° b) yes

2. 70°

3. Step 3 – 30°, Step 4 – 45°, Step 5 – 60°

4. Step 4

5. acute

6. 30°

WHAT ABOUT THIS? 7° per minute

PAGES 80–81

1. a) 16,400 ft b) 33,000 ft c) 262,500 ft

2. a) 27°F b) 43°F c) 7°F d) 81°F e) 24°F
   f) 50°F

3. 26,400 ft

4. 26,400 ft

PAGES 82–83

1. a) 56 b) 1½ or 1.5 c) -2 d) 750

2. a) 440 b) 840 c) 1060 d) 2040

3. a) about 50 miles b) about 6 minutes

PAGES 84–85

1. a) ten past six   b) twenty to nine
   c) ten past eleven   d) five to seven
   e) twenty-five past nine   f) five to twelve

2. a) twenty to two b) ten past four
   c) twenty-five past two d) five to five

3. 13:10, 14:40, 16:10

4. 20:55, 22:25, 23:55

PAGES 86–87

1. a) quarter turn counterclockwise and then another quarter turn counterclockwise
   b) quarter turn clockwise and then a quarter turn counterclockwise
   c) quarter turn clockwise and then a half turn (either clockwise or counterclockwise)

2. a) a right angle counterclockwise and then another right angle counterclockwise
   b) right angle clockwise and then a right angle counterclockwise
   c) a right angle clockwise and then two right angles (either clockwise or counterclockwise)

3. a) 90° counterclockwise and then 90° counterclockwise
   b) 270° counterclockwise and then 90° counterclockwise
   c) 270° counterclockwise and then 180° counterclockwise

4. a) yes b) no c) no d) yes

FLY A JET FIGHTER ANSWERS

Congratulations! Your squadron is ready for action! Check your answers here to see how well you did.

PAGES 90–91
1. a) 60 mph   b) 190 mph c) 230 mph
   d) 250 mph e) 540 mph f) 800 mph

2. 1,520 mph

3. a) 40 b) 80

4. a) 835 mph   b) 910 mph
   c) 1,445 mph d) 1,140 mph

PAGES 92–93
1. a) Chengdu J-10 b) Chengdu J-10
   c) F-22 Raptor   d) Chengdu J-10

2. Eurofighter Typhoon

3. a) 11.3 ft, b) 1.6 ft, c) 10.7 ft

4. a) 41,000 lb b) 9,300 lb c) 13,500 lb

PAGES 94–95
1. The turbojet was invented.

2. MiG 19

3. 16

4. 64

5. F-22 Raptor

6. 67

PAGES 96–97
1. Approximately: a) ¼ b) ⅓ c) ⅛ d) 1/12

2. Approximately: a) ¾ b) ⅔ c) ⅞ d) 11/12

3. a) 6 months b) 8 months c) 3 months
   d) 2 months e) 5 months

WHAT ABOUT THIS? The jet fighter spent
   4 months in air-to-air combat.

PAGES 98–99
1. 5

2. Theo, Emily, Deepa, Simon, Julia, Devon

3. Theo, Emily, Devon (male, female and male)

PAGES 100–101
1. a) seven o'clock
   b) half past nine
   c) quarter to eleven
   d) five to four
   e) twenty to five

2. a) 30 minutes b) 75 minutes c) 45 minutes
   d) 80 minutes

3. a) Physical training
   b) Morning briefing
   c) Studying weather conditions
   d) Simulated flight practice
   e) Flight grading
   f) Daily written exam

WHAT ABOUT THIS? A pilot will spend
   576 hours training.

PAGES 102–103

1. 2.4 miles

2. 90 miles per hour

3. a) 1 hour, b) ½ hour or 30 minutes
   c) ¼ hour or 15 minutes

4. a) 6 miles, b) 12 miles, c) 18 miles,
   d) 30 miles

5. a) 6 minutes b) 9 minutes

6. 4 minutes

WHAT ABOUT THIS? You would need to
   multiply it by 60. 12 x 60 = 720 mph.

PAGES 104–105

1. a) 870 mph b) 0.3-g c) 3 ft/s²
   d) -20 ft/s² e) 0.4 ft f) 480 ft
   g) 700 mph h) 1800 gallons i) 460 gallons
   j) 280 ft/s k) 0.65 ft l) 30 ft/s²

WHAT ABOUT THIS? The tanks have 250
   gallons of fuel left.

PAGES 106–107

1. a) 9 b) 4 c) 5 d) 5

2. a) square b) rhombus c) pentagon
   d) quadrilateral or trapezoid

3. a) 1, 3, 6, 10, 15, 21 b) yes

WHAT ABOUT THIS? Five more jets are
   needed to make the next largest square
   formation (nine in total).

PAGES 108–109

1. a) 1,600 N b) 2,400 N
   c) 3,200 N d) 4,000 N
   e) 4,800 N f) 5,600 N
   g) 6,400 N h) 7,200 N
   i) 8,000 N j) 8,800 N
   k) 9,600 N

2. a) 1,110 N b) 1,290 N
   c) 1,710 N d) 2,040 N

3. 180°

PAGES 110–111

1. a) 10 km/h b) 35 km/h c) 45 km/h
   d) 40 km/h e) 20 km/h f) 40 km/h

2. a) 12:00 and 16:30 b) 12:30 and 16:00 c) 9:30
   and 11:00 d) 10:00, 11:30, and 17:00

3. 08:00 North, 09:00 Northwest, 10:00 North,
   11:00 Northeast, 12:00 Southeast, 13:00 East,
   14:00 East, 15:00 Northeast, 16:00 Northwest,
   17:00 Southwest

4. 15:00

5. 15°

PAGES 112–113

1. a) (2, 6) b) (6, 5) c) (9, 6) d) (2, 3)
   e) (3, 2) f) (8, 3)

2. a) North b) Southwest c) West
   d) Northwest e) East f) Southeast

3. a) 4 squares b) 15½ squares c) 36½ squares

WHAT ABOUT THIS? 112/168 or ⅔

PAGES 114–115

1. a) right angle turn clockwise, half right angle
   turn clockwise, half right angle turn
   clockwise, two right angled turn (clockwise
   or counterclockwise)
   b) half right angle turn counterclockwise,
   half right angle turn counterclockwise, two
   right angled turns (clockwise or
   counterclockwise), right angle turn clockwise
   c) right angle counterclockwise, half right
   angle turn clockwise, right angle turn
   counterclockwise, half right angle turn
   clockwise.

2. a, b, and e pairs are parallel

WHAT ABOUT THIS? The jets in "A" are
   horizontal and the jets in "B" are vertical.

GLOSSARY

24-HOUR CLOCK
A clock that uses the numbers 0 to 23 to show the hours of a day. Midnight is 00:00 and midday is 12:00.

ACUTE
An angle that is less than 90 degrees.

ANGLE
An angle is an amount of turn. It is measured in degrees, such as 90°, which is also known as a right angle.

AREA
The area of a shape is the amount of surface it covers.

ASCEND
Ascend means going up.

COMPASS DIRECTION
The points found around a compass, including north, south, east and west.

CO-ORDINATES
Co-ordinates are used to show where something is on a map or graph. They are written like this (3, 4). The first number is how far across the horizontal axis and the second is how far up the vertical axis.

DECIMAL
This type of number uses a decimal point to show amounts that are less than a whole, such as 0.7, 0.42, and 6.83.

DESCEND
Descend means going down.

DIFFERENCE
The difference between two numbers can be found by subtracting the smaller number from the larger one.

FACE
A surface of a 3D shape. For example, a cube has six square-shaped faces.

FORMULA
A formula is a quick way of writing a mathematical rule.

FRACTION
A part of a whole. The number on the bottom (the denominator) tells you how many parts the whole has been split into. The number on the top (the numerator) tells you the number of equal parts being described.

HORIZONTAL
Straight across.

HORIZONTALLY
When something is going from side to side, like the horizon.

LINE GRAPH
A line graph shows information by using points and lines on a grid. Line graphs are often used to show changes over time.

MASS
How much matter there is in an object. Mass is measured using kilograms.

NEGATIVE NUMBERS
These are numbers that are less than zero. They are written using the minus sign.

OBTUSE
An angle that is greater than 90 degrees.

PARALLEL
Parallel lines stay the same distance apart along their entire length. No matter how long the lines are, they would never meet.

PERCENTAGE
A percentage is a special fraction which has a denominator of 100. For example, 42% = 42/100. Percent means "for every hundred."

PERIMETER

The perimeter is the length around the outside of a shape. It is measured in lengths, such as centimeters (cm) or meters (m).

PERPENDICULAR

When an object or a line is at right angles to another object or line.

PIE CHART

A pie chart is a type of graph that divides a circle in slices (sectors) of different sizes to show different amounts.

PRISM

A prism is a 3D shape that has the same cross-section throughout its length. For example, a triangular prism has a triangular cross-section.

PYRAMID

A 3D shape that has a polygon base, such as a square or triangle, and triangular sides, which lean inward and meet at the top in a point.

RATIO

Ratio is the relationship between two or more quantities, e.g., 3:4 which means 3 parts of one to 4 parts of another.

REFLECTIVE SYMMETRY

A shape or object has reflective symmetry when it has at least one mirror line that can split it into two reflected halves.

REFLEX

An angle that is greater than 180 degrees.

ROUND

To round a number to the nearest 10 is to say which multiple of 10 it is closest to. Numbers ending 1 to 4 are rounded down, while numbers ending 5 to 9 are rounded up.

SCALES

Scales are usually divided into equal sections and have a marker, such as an arrow, to show values. It is important to work out the value of each section to find the marked value.

SIMPLEST FORM

A fraction can be written in its simplest form by dividing the numerator (top number) and denominator (bottom number) by the largest number possible.

SIMPLIFY

This involves changing a fraction to an equivalent fraction that uses smaller numbers.

TIMELINE

A timeline is a line that shows events in chronological (date) order.

TRIANGULAR NUMBERS

A triangular number can be drawn as a pattern of dots to make a triangle. Examples include 1, 3, 6, and 10. The sequence follows a +2, +3, +4, +5... pattern.

VERTICAL

Straight up.

VERTICES

Vertices are the corners of a 3D shape. The singular of vertices is vertex.

VOLUME

The volume of a 3D shape is the amount of space it takes up, measured in cubes, such as cubic centimetres (cm³).

INDEX

© 2018 Quarto Publishing plc

First Published in 2018 by QEB Publishing,
an imprint of The Quarto Group.
6 Orchard Road, Suite 100,
Lake Forest, CA 92630
T: +1 949 380 7510
F: +1 949 380 7575
www.QuartoKnows.com

A CIP record for this book is available
from the Library of Congress.

ISBN 978 1 68297 302 8

Manufactured in Guangdong, China CC112017

9 8 7 6 5 4 3 2 1

MIX
Paper from
responsible sources
FSC® C008047
FSC
www.fsc.org